LAUGHING LOST

IN THE

MOUNTAINS

LAUGHING LOST

IN THE

MOUNTAINS

Poems of Wang Wei

TRANSLATIONS BY

TONY BARNSTONE

WILLIS BARNSTONE

XU HAIXIN

Critical Introduction by Willis Barnstone & Tony Barnstone

University Press of New England / Hanover & London

University Press of New England,

Hanover, New Hampshire 03755

Printed in Canada   5 4 3 2

CIP data appear at the end of the book

Dry-brush ink drawings by Willis Barnstone.

FOR

AYAME FUKUDA

AND

SARAH HANDLER

C O N T E N T S

ACKNOWLEDGMENTS

Some of the poems in this collection first appeared in the following journals, sometimes in earlier versions: from *Artful Dodge*, Lazy about Writing Poems; East River Moon; Red Peonies; Drifting on the Lake; and About Old Age, in Answer to a Poem by Zhang Shaofu; from *The Centennial Review*, Written in My Garden in the Spring; Lady Pan; and Missing the Loved One; from *The Literary Review*, Moaning about My White Hair; Composed on Horseback for My Younger Brother Cui the Ninth on His Departure to the South; Going to the Country in the Spring; The Stillness of Meditation; Deep South Mountain; In the Mountains; Night Over the Huai River; For Someone Far Away; Lakeside Pavilion; and Winter Night, Writing About My Emotion; from *Nimrod*, Suffering from Heat; Weeping for Ying Yao; Visiting the Mountain Courtyard of the Distinguished Monk Tanxing at Ganghua Monastery; and Written When Climbing the City Tower North of the River; from *Occident*, Answering the Poem Su Left in My Lan Tian Country House, on Visiting and Finding Me Not Home; Clean Landscape after the Storm; and a Young Lady's Spring Thoughts; from *Practices of the Wind*, Drifting on the Lake; Sitting Alone on an Autumn Night; and To My Cousin Qiu, Military Supply Official; and from *Quarry West*, White Pebble Shoal.

March 1991
Bloomington, Indiana   W. B.
Berkeley, California   T. B.

Empty Mountain

An empty mountain. Rain. A voice. White clouds.

On the *empty mountain* the poet has been meditating, and now he is empty like the mountain. A sudden *rain* refreshes. Perhaps the *voice* is the laughter of the poet by himself or a chat with a woodcutter who will put him up for the night. The poet listens to the whine of cicadas, notes with sadness his balding white head, and reaches a lodge or spends the night at a temple where, drinking and talking to a friend, he is happy. He will be ready again next morning to walk in the mountains, which are so far from the human world of imperial court and frontier battles that they dissolve like *white clouds*. He has an appointment with white clouds, and there, once again, he will study nonbeing.

With these four elements—*empty mountain, rain, voice, white clouds*—we have the scene of many of Wang Wei's poems. The *empty mountain* is the poet's place of solitude, where he will try to escape from illusory things of the phenomenal world and go into *sunyata*, the principle of Buddhist universal emptiness; *rain* is a sudden commingling in nature of heavens and earth, is refreshing and transforming like illumination; *voice* is the encounter of friendship in the wilderness; the eternal flux of *white clouds* in which the world dissolves may be the entry to enlightenment and nothingness.

Yet for all of the recurrent symbolism and hints of transcendence, Wang Wei did not write formally religious poetry.

He was a devout Mahayana Buddhist, who followed a Chan (Zen) master, yet no sutras, no hymns, no doctrine enter in his poems. Like one of his poetic counterparts in the West, the Spanish mystical poet Saint John of the Cross, Wang Wei rarely uses theological terms in his poetry. But his work does suggest an allegorical interpretation (as did that of John of the Cross), in this instance to convey Taoist and Buddhist notions. Referring to Wang's nondidactic poems, in which images convey immediate and not merely symbolic meaning, Burton Watson writes succinctly:

The second type of Buddhist poetry is that in which the philosophical meaning lies much farther below the surface. The imagery functions on both the descriptive and the symbolic levels at once, and it is not often possible to pin down the exact symbolic content of an image. These poems make no doctrinal point or deliver no sermon; they are Buddhist only in their general tone or outlook, and in fact if one were unaware of the author's identity, or did not know that he was a believer, one might never think of them as Buddhist at all—which, of course, from the Buddhist point of view, would mark them as the highest type. (Watson, 1971, p. 171)

In his elegant simplicity Wang Wei needed few words to paint his world. Of course, he was also a painter—the legendary father of "literary" landscape painting—and his poems are often described as spoken paintings, his paintings as silent poems. Robert Payne observes that he "can evoke a whole landscape in a single line" (Payne, p. 150). Indeed, an elegant poverty of characters is his strength. With few words he achieves a quiet lucidity. In our century Wang Wei has been translated more often than any other Chinese poet, and perhaps a reason for his appeal to English-speaking readers lies in the absolute clarity of his imagery. We find a minimalist presentation that is paradoxically resonant with allusions and levels of interpretation. Similarly, his range is limited to the modest events of his life. He speaks of the days of a reluctant official or of a hermit in Virgilian retreat; of banishment; of friendship, with its encounters and separations; and of nature, with its many personal and metaphysical implications. As for the last, he returns relentlessly to themes of seclusion and meditation in the mountains, in all of their seasons.

Like spare forms of a Ming table and in contrast to late Qing ornament, Wang Wei's lines are clean and with no decoration whatsoever. Though the same characters occur again and again, each austerely compact line is an amazingly fresh insight. By subtle shifts in syntax and implied speaker, each evocation of moon or mountain is sensitively distinct. He has the genius of profound simplicity. In a voice, a particle, one bell in the mountain, or a shuddering leaf, he sees, as William Blake saw in his "grain of sand," a universe. Much quieter than Blake, there is, nevertheless, more than a coincidence in the fact of two figures who were of distinction in poetry and painting. Their poems shine with primal images, with undertones in one case of Taoist spontaneity and paradox, and in the other of mystical whimsy. To an alert reader a poem by Wang or by Blake slides easily into social or cosmic allegory.

Wang Wei did not need to go beyond the immediacy of his life to find his some four hundred poems. Although confined to his obsessions of the court and nature, his imagination was deep within its restricted scope. He wrote about what he saw—a dismal court life, frontier adventures, a hermitage, a friend, his own failures—and was happiest when he perceived and read life through nature.

Nature and Vision

As a nature poet Wang Wei resembles to an astonishing degree the Spanish poet Antonio Machado (1875–1939), who, like Wang, keeps the purity of the clear nature image, the quietude, the emotional control, and the resignation to plain beauty. In each poet, war, exile, and the tedium of their professions play a part, but it is into and with nature that their spirits escape and merge. Often it is enough for the poet to convey personal feelings through the depiction of nature alone. A single element in nature is synecdochic of the whole human situation. In referring to a separation, the poet conveys both the season and physical distance of their separation by asking what is happening to nature. Wang Wei asks,

> When you left, had the cold plum blossomed
> by her carved window?
>> (from "Thoughts from a Harbor on the Yellow River")

and Machado asks,

> Already the bees
> are sipping thyme and rosemary.
> Are the plum trees in bloom?   (Machado, p. 73)[1]

At times Machado unexpectedly seems to fulfill a common goal of Chinese poetry, and particularly of Wang Wei, which is to objectify idea and emotion by finding a metaphorical equivalent in nature, to see everything through a scene. As Wang uses the empty mountain to evoke the poet alone in nature, and by extension the poet's own solitude, Machado also infers the poet's solitude by visualizing a Sorian landscape in which wind inhabits the solitariness of the fields. Full of movement, season, aroma, as the meadow is alive and happy, the poet, by implication, is similarly so because of his solitary involvement in nature, with which he is in invisible harmony.

> The blue mountain, the river, the erect
> coppery staffs of slender aspens,
> and the white of almond trees on the hill.
> O snow in flower and butterfly on the tree!
> With the aroma of bean plants, the wind
> runs in the joyful solitude of the fields   (Machado, pp. 94–95)[2]

Wang an official, Machado a teacher in a rural *instituto*, both poets find their eyes in nature. They were not scribes of the imagination, like Dante, but of their daily and nightly vision. They tended to dream—but not nocturnal dreams associated with sleep and wild fantasy. Theirs was a reverie of ordinary landscapes, which their minds transposed as they gazed at them with eyes wide open. In nature Wang—and later Machado—found a literal script for his vision.

The model for Wang Wei's pastoral retreat was Tao Qian (365–427), a poet from the period known as the Six Dynasties. Tao Qian (also called Tao Yuanming) gave up his official's career early to retire to a life of Taoist simplicity in the country. He became a farmer and experienced the joys of country life as well as its hardships. His poems were plain. He had rejected the ornate diction and rhetoric of his time as Wang Wei similarly avoided the impersonality and ornamental complexity of poets of the early Tang. Wang Wei has many allusions to Tao Qian—more than to any other earlier figure—and his first well-known poem, "Song of Peach Tree Spring," is in imitation of Tao Qian's poetic narration of a Taoist paradise, "Peach Blossom Spring."

Though both Tao Qian and Wang Wei wrote poems of eremitic seclusion, Wang Wei retreated to nature, but he retained his official posts till the end. And even his "cottage" was the mansion of a country gentleman, not that of a recluse or an impoverished peasant. (Tu Fu's modest cottage at Chengdu, celebrated in those poems of companionship with Li Po, was also an elegant country villa.) Wang's commitment was ostensibly weak. Pauline Yu perceptively observes that in his failure to make an unambiguous move he hedged (Yu, 1980, p. 46). Therein lies the real personal

drama of the poet: his wavering between urbanity and self-immersi[on]
nature. Wang's weakness was his humanity. It made him painfully
sitive to conflicting drives throughout his life and cast him as a
soul" of literary history. Unlike Tao Qian's monolithic retirement, Wang
Wei retained an ambiguity in his life and poems that intensified each new
declaration of pastoral discovery.

The Old Man in the Mountain

In most of Wang Wei's mountain poems, the poet is present, and that
very presence is essential to the poem's message. We understand his pres-
ence, however, not through the use of pronouns, which occur rarely in
classical Chinese poetry, but by context and by the use of verbs of human
action. In a few significant poems there is an absence in the center of
the poem: the narrator is missing. Here the poet's art is not to intrude
overtly. Although invisibly present and intensely personal, like William
Carlos Williams in his objectivist poetry, Wang Wei has written himself
out of the poem. In "Luan Family Rapids" we feel this absence:

> In the windy hiss of autumn rain
> shallow water fumbles over stones.
> Waves dance and fall on each other:
> a white egret startles up, then drops.

Only by deduction do we conjure up the poet alone in the landscape,
observing the scene and writing the lines. Whereas the poet is physically
present in other poems, here he is no more than a convention, a con-
vention of an implicit observer, selecting details, making judgments. We
know this role because we read Wang Wei in the context of the greater
corpus of his work. In the same way that the unidentified "you" in a se-
quence of Petrarchan laments is glossed by the tradition and other related
poems as referring to the poet's recalcitrant lover or Beauty, in these lines
Wang Wei's escape to a pastoral landscape is such a prime topos in his
work—and in Chinese poetry in general—that we understand the pres-
ence of a speaker. We visualize an old man in the mountain, meditating
on nature.

As the observer in the poem is intuitively suggested through his ab-
sence, the movement and meaning of the poem is presented through the
absence of connectives. The poem's events are simply registered—the
hissing of rain in the wind, the tumult of water over stones, the dance

and fall of waves, the startling and settling of the egret—but they are not interpreted for the reader. Instead, the reader must do what the poet has already implicitly done: interpret the phenomena, understand the parallelism of movement and sound that take place from line to line. The aesthetic behind the parallelism of these nature elements is common to Chinese poetry, in which parallelism of syntax, image, and meaning is a device preferred to the explicitness of metaphor and simile in Western poetics.

In "Luan Family Rapids" we perceive an active element of causality: the rain feeds the stream as the waves startle the egret. This causality is circular. The rain feeding the stream is itself created by the flow and eventual evaporation of water flowing oceanward. Similarly, the egret may be startled by the slap of waves or may itself be the cause of the splash by its sudden flight. This circularity is reflected in other parallelisms of motion that occur in these four lines: the water falls through the air, then passes over stones; the waves rise and fall over the stones as does the egret in the air. Another kind of parallelism in the poem is the syntactical mirroring of the first and second lines. The first line creates an emphatic and onomatopoetic evocation of the sound of the wind by repetition of the initial character [颯颯] (*sa sa*), meaning, "sough, sough." (We try to replicate this device of repetition for emphasis and onomatopoeia through assonance: "*In* the *windy hiss*.") In the second line, Wang parallels the first line by repetition of the initial character [淺淺] (*qian qian*), meaning "shallow, shallow." Here, the repetition is emphatic rather than onomatopoetic.

At this point the poem seems transparent. On one level it is an artifact of interlocking relations that one apprehends merely as an aesthetically pleasing observation of nature. On closer inspection, however, the lyric reflects certain commonplaces of Buddhism, and we also discover a didactic purpose behind the poem. The poem suggests precisely that causality that in Buddhism locks one into the profane world of *mutability*, causing all life to spin endlessly in the Great Wheel of Being, perpetuating rebirth and misery.

The alternate, transcendent Buddhist vision infers the *unity* of all beings (mirrored here in the unity of the disparate aspects of nature), the oneness of all being that underlies reality and constitutes escape from the cycle of birth and rebirth. It is appropriate that this oneness is reflected in the rise and fall of the water and the bird, since the rise and fall of human breath is the prime unit of meditation, the method of achieving oneness.

As with the topos of the Book of Nature in Renaissance England, the transcendental in Wang Wei is to be read in the phenomena of the natural world. One approaches the ineffable obliquely, as in *Paradise Lost*, where Adam reads God through his creations. Adam speaks of

> The scale of nature set
> From center to circumference, whereon
> In contemplation of created things
> By steps we may ascend to God.
>
> (Milton, *Paradise Lost*, Book V, lines 509–12)

The transcendental sign that unifies nature for Wang Wei is distinguished from the Western sign in that in Buddhism the sign implies an absence, not a presence. Through the contemplation of the unity of all things, we may revert to that primordial absence, particularly in nature, which is viewed as closer to the absent center than is the dusty busy world of people. The knowledge that all is illusion is a step toward escape from the mutable world to the emptiness and perfect stillness of nirvana.

The apparent absence of the poet in this and a few other poems allows the reader to meditate on nature in the poem, with no distracting intrusion by the author. The poem then is a pure text of nature, worthy of contemplation. We have here an equation in which the poem is nature, the word is its object, and at the moment of contemplation there is no distinction between them. In a very real sense, then, the medium (a formal technique of conveying nature without authorial presence) is the message in Wang Wei. His poetic techniques produce an artifact whose proper contemplation can itself be the catalyst, a Zen koan, for entering a state of *ekstasis*. As we move into meditation, we may become aware of the unstated presence of the poet who, through his rigorously personal and subtle observations, has led us this far.

The absence of overt connections between lines—and the occasional apparent absence of a speaker in Wang Wei's poetry—may sometimes lead some readers to misapprehend the poetry. Another reason for misapprehension lies in the elusive ties between a nature (described significantly) and the speaker, which very often have only a paratactic tie (that is, they appear in sequence without conjunctions to connect them). In the poem "Return to Wang River," the poet appears in the poem twice:

> Bells stir in the mouth of the gorge.
> Few fishermen and woodcutters are left.
> Far off in the mountains is twilight.

Alone I come back to white clouds.
Weak water chestnut stems can't hold still.
Willow catkins are light and blow about.
To the east is a rice paddy, color of spring grass.
I close the thorn gate, seized by grief.

A landscape is described, through which, one understands, the poet is returning to his cottage. The epiphany of grief in the last line is the key. On first glance a Western reader might complain that the last line has not been prepared for, not fleshed out with clues, not justified. The poem appears to deal not with any specific trauma of the narrator but with the mere description of a landscape. Yet nature in Wang Wei, as we have seen, is not only what it appears to be. Like the "book of nature," in Milton and Emerson, Wang's landscape is resonant with symbolic messages that can lead to transcendence. Wang's is also an emotional landscape. And so it is perfectly right for the speaker to be seized by grief.

In much of Wang's poetry the topos of the old man in the mountain defines both the speaker and the scene. In this lyric the poet places himself explicitly within the landscape, but there would be a failure of meaning were there no external reference or hermeneutic to unravel the images. In Wang Wei this contextualization occurs primarily through allusion to ancient Buddhist, Taoist, or poetic texts, but sometimes it occurs through an intertextual glossing within his own work. In this instance the title "Return to Wang River" brings us quickly into relation with the *Wang River Sequence*, Wang's famous series of poems, each of which describes a different place in his Wang River estate, the country retreat where he would escape from city duties into Buddhist meditation. That he speaks of a return to Wang River establishes a scene in which the poet is in transition between two worlds.

This poem again works through a direct, unelaborated presentation of images embedded in a series of parallelistic couplets. The bells call the fishermen and woodcutters back after a day's work. The lonely sound of the bell is in emotional accord with the scarcity of people. The distance of the mountains parallels the poet's Rilkean isolation in the same way that twilight (day's transition into night) suggests the poet's transition from the peopled court to the meditative world of his retreat. The next four lines work similarly. The water chestnuts and willow catkins are blown about by winds, they "can't hold still," while the rice paddies shine bright with new life. But, like the weak plants, the poet is still attached to things of the world and, made lonely by the desolate landscape, has not achieved the emancipatory stillness for which he has come to his retreat. The rice paddy, "color of spring grass," speaks a climactic moment as the last statement about nature, leading him to confront himself. The vibrant rice signifies new life, either in ironic contrast to the poet's inability to give up the life of the court, which is so often Wang Wei's grief, or as a symbol of hope that, after the poet has learned again in stillness, renewal will come.

Through a process of meditation, then, a synthesis of the apparently disparate elements in the poem is achieved, and the dramatic summation—"I close the thorn gate, seized by grief"—is in the end justified. In the same way that nature implies the invisible presence of the narrator in "Luan Family Rapids," so the phenomena of nature suggest the poet's emotions well before the final expression of pain in "Return to Wang River." The poem feels right, whether or not the labyrinth of parallel symbols is perceived, for the consummately subtle choice of images and meaningful resonances produces an intuitive understanding.

Deep Nature in the West and a Chinese *Paysage* of Symbols

In the West we find a similar poetics operating on both sides of the Atlantic. Once again, Antonio Machado, most Chinese of Spanish poets, is uncannily close to Wang Wei. Machado is the alien observer whose gaze leads us through the clear images of a village night scene in "Summer Night."

> A beautiful summer night.
> The tall houses leave
> their balcony shutters open
> to the wide plaza of the old village.
> In the large deserted square,
> stone benches, burning bush and acacias
> trace their black shadows
> symmetrically on the white sand.
> In its zenith, the moon; in the tower,
> the clock's illuminated globe.
> I walk through this ancient village,
> alone, like a ghost.

It is a poem of parallelisms, of objects and their shadows, the moon in its zenith and the illuminated globe of the clock in its tower, and, in typically Chinese comparison of external scene with inner condition, these beautiful, luminous, shadowy images of emptiness are an analogue of the poet, transient, passing by like a ghost.

Or consider this poem by James Wright:

Lying in a Hammock at William Duffy's Farm in Pine Island, Minnesota

Over my head, I see the bronze butterfly,
Asleep on the black trunk,
Blowing like a leaf in green shadow.
Down the ravine behind the empty house,
The cowbells follow one another
Into the distances of the afternoon.
To my right,
In a field of sunlight between two pines,
The droppings of last year's horses
Blaze up into golden stones.
I lean back, as the evening darkens and comes on.
A chicken hawk floats over, looking for home.
I have wasted my life.

(Wright, p. 114)

The poem evokes a pattern of deep images loosely associated with twilight, the return to one's proper home, new life, and the renewal of sleep. The butterfly, the cattle, the horses, and the hawk all have their proper places, in contrast to the poet, who is lying in someone else's hammock. Even last year's horse droppings have a place in the cycle of things as they are resurrected now as golden stones. So the shock of the final line, as in the last line of the Chinese poem "Return to Wang River," is mitigated on rereading, when these suggestions become clear. A second reading, revealing clues of home, permanence, impermanence, and emptiness, should indeed prepare the reader for the devastating and acutely self-critical last line, where all of the sensible activities of nature are contrasted with the speaker's uncertainties.

Wright's poem is the work of an American poet with many foreign influences, including Chinese, which is testimony to the increasing penetration of Chinese—and Japanese—aesthetics into American poetry. There are generations of poets representing a persistent thread of Asian poetics active in the American field. The thread stretches from the early *Imagiste* experimentations of T. E. Hulme and Amy Lowell, Ezra Pound and H. D., from early translations by Pound and Arthur Waley, through Wallace Stevens's lush chinoiserie and William Carlos Williams's early work, his "no ideas but in things," and his later translations in *The Cassia Tree*. We see the thread surface in the Black Mountain poetry of Denise Levertov and in the Deep Image of Wright and Robert Bly, in the Beat poetry of Gary Snyder and most recently in poets like Sam Hamill and Robert Hass. Behind these movements and writers are the poems and the poetics and sometimes the philosophy of China and Japan.

The impact of Asia also reflects an increasing internationalism of American poetry, largely as a result of translation. Though some of the means by which Chinese poetry achieves its effects may be unfamiliar to Western readers, this is less and less so as American poetry appropriates what it can from Asia—almost exclusively through translation and commentary—and fashions the Chinese image into a Western equivalent.

Wang Wei's poetic landscape is a mountain range of symbols. Like the landscapes of the Romantic imagination, it is in intimate contact with the poet's emotions and is both the setting and the agency for the poet's revelation. The elements in this natural world, while specific and meticulously observed, are selected carefully to resonate symbolically against one another.

In some poems, as we have seen, they resonate not only with each other but with other texts. Allusion in Chinese poetry is, of course, the bane of translators, who must either incorporate explanations into the poem or employ lengthy notes to give the reader something approaching the poem's full impact. But allusion is at the prosodic and philosophical core of Chinese poetry.

The use (and reuse) of traditional symbols in Chinese poetry points up an essential difference from the West, with its cult of the individual in art, the "anxiety of influence," or the basically Oedipal relation of Western artists to their mentors. The East, with its deep-rooted effacement of the individual and Confucian respect for authority, is at the other end of this spectrum of anxiety. The Renaissance doctrine of imitation, in which writers created versions of classical texts, was less a process of imitating than of rewriting. In China a practice of imitation also was active, but unlike the Western one, which intrinsically carries the sense of diminishment by virtue of being an imitation of a paradigmatic original, imitation in China was conceived more as a means of honoring the masters. It is usually accomplished through allusion rather than actual appropriation—and imitation and allusion are not neurotically obsessed, in the eyes of author or critic, with a nervous concern for originality.

Wang Wei's poetry is a personal statement about intimate occasions of his life, yet imitation of and respect for earlier writers and their symbol systems are everywhere evident in his work. In Wang Wei the natural world is a *paysage* of ancient symbols made new by the specific context of the poem. Thus, while the poetic project is sanctioned by antiquity, these symbols are personalized by their use in this poetry of intimate occasions. His main system of symbols derives from his retreat in the forest and hills.

Wang Wei's pastoral awakenings occur in solitude and in a realm of quietude. If at times he attains an ecstasy of stillness in his poems, it is in part because he has temporarily thrown off everyday clamor. The process of ecstasy is a movement from *enstasis* to *ekstasis*, from "inself" to "other self," from a known condition to the paradisaical oblivion of the unknown. Because Wang Wei himself moves from one condition of life to another, from city to mountain, from anxiety to peace, from willed activity to vulnerability, from bafflement to discovery, he is able to hear a woodcutter's human voice or a hibiscus flowering in the calm of absolute silence.

Wang's seclusion at his Wang River estate (where he went to meditate in his "cottage" at the foot of Deep South Mountain), his official posts, banishment, incarceration, his reading, and his religious meditations are the facts of his life that provide virtually all of the material for his poems. Let us say some words, then, about this external source of Wang Wei's poetry, the poet's life.

An Uneventful Life

It is often written that Wang Wei had an uneventful life; more, that his life had little to do with his poetry, since he couched his poems in impersonality, and indeed that his poetry, to use Eliot's term, was an "escape from personality." In the same vein it is said that as a poet he was merely a catalyst for emotions, impassive before nature. To use the frequent Buddhist analogy, he was just one thing among the things of nature, a mirror in which the world shone. All of these notions have a tempting general truth to them. Applied to Wang Wei, as they frequently are, they are deeply erroneous and at best misleading. Though understated, quiet, and often serene, Wang Wei was neither impersonal nor impassive before routine city life or nature. On the contrary, he was actively engaged in his official routines and in his spiritual quest in the countryside. His poems, as well as those of Li Bai (Li Po) and Du Fu (Tu

Fu), initiate the reassertion of a confessional mode, however couched in convention they may appear to be. All of this becomes clear when we compare biography and poems. In effect, Wang Wei's life was the subtext of his poems. One might contend that we need not seek additional bio-graphical sources to augment a reading of the poems because the poems themselves provide the vital context of his every day. The few reliable facts of a life and a period do, however, remain essential and help clarify the many references.[3]

Wang Wei was a poet, painter, calligrapher, and musician. He was also a bureaucrat, whose first position at a very young age was assis-tant minister of music in the palace of the Emperor Xuanzong, popularly known as Minghuang, the Brilliant Emperor. The major poets in the High Tang (early eighth century) worked as poet-officials in the bureau-cracy. Especially during the Tang dynasty, the state encouraged gifted poets through examinations and sinecures. There were actually elaborate imperial examinations in poetry, the *jinshi*, a tradition that continued for all bureaucrats until early in the twentieth century. Much of the artistic splendor of the Tang, the zenith of Chinese poetry, may be attributed to the active encouragement of the arts by the government. Wang Wei's poetry was itself the object of strong praise in verse by the emperor. Li Bai, Du Fu, and Wang Wei are the best-known poets of the Tang, but they were three in a multitude. On the basis of earlier collections, the *Complete Tang Poetry* (*Chuan Tang Shi*) was compiled in the eighteenth century and contains more than 48,000 poems by some 2,200 poets. Professor Liu Wu-chi records commonplace enthusiasm for the period:

In the T'ang dynasty (618–906), China became the hub of the Eastern world, and all roads from Asia led to Ch'ang-an, its most magnificent metropolis. This was an era of brilliant intellectual and literary activities unsurpassed by any other period in Chinese history. The splendor and the subsequent decline of the T'ang period are reflected in its poetry. T'ang China, like Elizabethan England, was virtually a nation of singing birds. (Liu, 1966, p. 69)

Wang Wei was born in Shanxi province in 699 or 701. There is much debate about the actual dates of his birth and death. Since biographical sources are in conflict, it is best to go with Stephen Owen's sensible ar-ticulation: "He was born either in 699 or 701 and died in 759 or 761" (Owen, 1977, p. 29). His family was from two powerful clans: on his father's side the Taiyuan Wang clan of middle-level government officials; on his mother's, the Boling Qui clan, especially prominent as *littérateurs*. Their families were among the "Seven Great Surnames," families considered by the earlier Emperor Gaozong as powerful enough to be a danger to the realm and the object of a ban in 659 against intermarriage—a ban obviously ignored.

Precocious as a poet and musician, Wang Wei passed the provincial examination in 719 and two years later went to the capital, Chang'an, where he passed the crucial *jinshi*, "presented scholar," exam. In the *jinshi*, the candidate was tested on his knowledge of the classics and ethical issues and above all was obliged to compose poetry in the *fu* and *shi* (verse) forms. In any case, aided evidently by the patronage of imperial princes, Wang was appointed to the good position of assistant minister of music. His skills as a *pipa* player were also recorded. The *pipa*, a long stringed instrument resembling and sounding like the Greek bouzouki, was one of those popular instruments that came into Han China during the Tang period, from Turkistan and the Near East by way of the Silk Route.

Despite the artistic glory of the dynasty, the period was also, typically, marked by intrigues and ferocious power struggles within the imperial family for the throne and other positions and between the throne and would-be outside contenders. The emperor's grandmother, Empress Wu, had usurped the throne in 690, deposing his uncle Jongzong. At twenty-eight the emperor put down an attempted coup by his aunt, the Princess Taiping, daughter of Empress Wu, and killed the members of that group. In such an ambience, barely two years after his appointment Wang Wei found himself accused of a minor indiscretion—he may have permitted a musician to perform a forbidden dance—and was demoted to the post of granary administrator and sent far off to Qizhou in Shandong province in what amounted to banishment from the capital. So he turned to the old tradition of exile poetry, which Li Bai and Du Fu were also to practice and in which he was to excel.

> *On Being Demoted and Sent Away to Qizhou*
>
> How easy for a lowly official to offend
> and now I'm demoted and must go north.
> In my work I sought justice
> but the wise emperor disagreed.
> I pass houses and roads by the riverside
>   and villages deep in a sea of clouds.
> Even if one day I come back,
> white age will have invaded my hair.

Wang Wei is distressed and speaks with unusual candor of his personal grievance. He thinks himself a victim—his disgrace was probably the result of his protectors falling out of favor—and even the emperor, he suggests with scarcely disguised irony, does not, despite his "wisdom," understand. He broods about an uncertain future of wasted years and distress in which "white age" will have invaded his hair. His official career is dashed for more than a decade.

Another exile poem, "Seeing Zu Off at Qizhou," is an extraordinary example of another kind of candor, that of affection and sorrow at the separation from a close friend.

> *Seeing Zu Off at Qizhou*
>
> Only just now we met and laughed
> yet here I'm crying to see you off.
> In the prayer tent we are broken.
> The dead city intensifies our grief.
> Coldly the remote mountains are clean.
> Dusk comes. The long river races by.
> You undo the rope, are already gone.
> I stand for a long time, looking.

Here Wang Wei uses a strategy of *movement* in nature, in the friend's departure, in the passage of time of the last line, which continues the poem after its closure and contrasts with his own static exile. He stands, looking indefinitely, as if forever. The poet and his friend are alive as long as there is movement, as in the first couplet, when laughter and crying reflect the shudder of emotion in the laughing throat and weeping eyes. The parallel flux in nature is revealed as twilight comes and the river races away. In the final couplet the undone rope gives freedom to the departing friend, paralysis to the speaker. The other major symbol of the poet's motionless posture is the "dead city," an epithet of his exile, intensifying his grief. In Wang Wei's poems, the mountains are almost always representations of refuge and consolation. Now they are coldly remote. Nature operates normally, fulfilling its mission of defining distance and movement—the river races by to take his friend away—and so conspires to leave the speaker even more abandoned. This poem is a historical moment in which the good past and much of the future is mirrored in the moment of awakening to absence and pain. The recognition is a negative epiphany, for, in this brief interlude, sudden knowledge leads not to illumination or freedom but to grief. The poem is itself almost a late mirror of the famous Greek quatrain attributed (probably erroneously) to Sappho.

Alone

The moon and Pleiades
are set. Midnight,
and time spins away.
I lie in bed, alone.   (Barnstone, 1988, p. 67)

In these Lesbian lyrics—and it is certain that the verses are in the Aeolian Greek of the island of Lesbos—the moon, the stars have all gone to their proper destination. Only time goes on, purposelessly, while the narrator lies in bed, in her solitude, contemplating the cosmic movement of heavenly bodies to their meaningful end and, by contrast, recognizing her own unfulfilled condition of empty stasis. No lover is mentioned, but the notion of desolate separation is as intense as in the Chinese lyric. Both poems reveal the quintessential ecstasy of pain. As time is measured only by movement, so negative ecstasy is measured by movement from one time of pain into another, from one condition of knowledge into another.

There is uncertainty about the next ten years of Wang Wei's life. At some point he married. His wife died around 730. Thereafter, he took a Buddhist vow of celibacy, which he maintained for thirty years, till the end of his life. It is also said that he became a vegetarian. The tragic loss of his young wife, which decisively altered his life, is apparently alluded to in the poem "To Repay My Friends for Their Visit," which begins dejectedly, "Oh, I am not yet dead, despairing over this life alone!" In this same period he became deeply committed to Buddhism and was the disciple of a Zen master, Daoguang. When his teacher died some ten years later, in 739, Wang Wei recorded as part of the pagoda inscription in honor of Daoguang, "For ten years I sat at his feet and obediently received his instruction."

Wang Wei remained about four years as a banished functionary in Qizhou and then wandered in the eastern provinces for some years. During the period of travel he visited friends in Taoist and Buddhist monasteries, which he records in many poems. He speaks ideally of the life of the monks, of their tranquility and removal from urban conflict and noise, and of the great beauty of their retreats in the mountains. Already the personal conflict was brewing, never to end, between his own call to the city and court and his desire for spiritual peace in the countryside. At some time he acquired his estate at Wang River, perhaps during this decade or after his formal return to Chang'an. Much of his mature poetry concerns his life there, his escape to the reality of disengagement and the study of nonbeing and illumination. But it always remained a temporary escape, not a definitive acceptance. He occupied a salaried official position virtually throughout his life.

The conflict in Wang Wei between the draw of urban politics and materialism as opposed to abandonment to the spirit in nature recalls the parallel unresolved struggle between body and soul that permeates the poetry of the great English meditative poets. George Herbert, John Donne, and Andrew Marvell never tamed the dragon and the angel. Perhaps it is precisely because of the vacillation between worldly and spiritual concerns that Wang's city poems carry such a cargo of pathos and longing, and his nature poems are inevitably revelatory, a series of wakenings to Taoist quietude and simplicity.

> *Drifting on the Lake*
> Autumn is crisp and the firmament far,
> especially far from where people live.
> I look at cranes on the sand
> and am immersed in joy when I see mountains beyond
> the clouds.
> Dusk inks the crystal ripples.
> Leisurely the white moon comes out.
> Tonight I am with my oar, alone, and can do
> everything,
> yet waver, not willing to return.

He writes as if astonished before this peaceable beauty. Yet while immersed in joy and the vision of mountains beyond the clouds, waver he will. Wang Wei did go back to the court at Chang'an in 734 when, through the intervention of his friend Zhang Jiuling, then prime minister, he returned to favor. He was appointed to a responsible position, advisor on the right, a post that required him to reproach the emperor for oversights. The return and resumption of his career as an aspiring yet (if the poems are true) reluctant official all occurred presumably before his hair turned completely white.

After three years in Chang'an there was another power struggle, and in 737 Wang Wei was conveniently kicked upstairs and out of the way; that is, he was given a modest promotion and sent to Liangzhou at the northwest frontier, in present-day Gansu province. This time Wang did not consider his remote post a banishment. He was a censor. His duty was to report on wrongdoings in any quarter. But above all it was an adventure, a distinct one, leading to unexpected voices in the poems. A sense of the lonely uncertainty appears in the following quatrain as his friend Yuan prepares to cross the Yang Pass into the wilderness.

Seeing Yuan Off on His Official Trip to Anxi

Morning rain in Weicheng dampens the dusty ground.
Willow trees give the inn courtyard a fresh greenness.
Why not drink one more bowl of wine?
Beyond Yang Pass there are only strangers.

Wang finds an ingenious way of evoking the immense solitude of the Gobi and its lurking dangers. First he speaks of morning rain on the parched ground and of willow trees that give the fresh greenness of life to an inn courtyard. But beyond the scene-setting and evocation of essential nature there is, as always in poems to friends, a parallelism of nature and life, and in this instance nature beyond the pass will contain ominous danger for life itself. So why not share another drink now? As earth without water and life becomes desert, when Yuan crosses Yang Pass into the Gobi, there will be no one to give him the welcome draught of friendship. There will be only strangers and perhaps, as we shall see in the next poem, something far worse. These lines prefigure the fuller treatment of the same scene and frontier conditions as he says goodbye to another friend, Ping Danran.

Saying Goodbye to Ping Danran, Overseer

You don't know the road after Yang Pass.
Only now have you joined the governor of the border lands
where yellow clouds blot out spring colors
and frontier sadness blows from a painted horn.
It takes years to get through the Dry Sea of the Gobi
    Desert
where the Forked River flows on the other side of
    the border post.
When you set out as an envoy to the Tatars be careful:
You may be drinking from a bowl made from the skull
    of the Yuezhi king.

In the life of internal exile at the border where "yellow sands blot out spring colors and frontier sadness blows from a painted horn," despite excitement of the new region, beyond the pass the unknown may mean death. In that "Dry Sea of the Gobi Desert" that "takes years to get through," be careful, Wang warns, or one may end up in the hands of the Tatars, like the Yuezhi king whose skull was made into a drinking bowl.

The poet was back in Chang'an in less than two years, where he confronted a new tangle of rising factions. In 739 he was the court censor, and for the next seventeen years, until the An Lushan rebellion, he occupied a series of similar positions, some in Chang'an and at least one in the south, where he was supervisor of the examinations. Through discretion and moderate flattery he kept aloof from the major political conflicts. He also apparently lost interest and consequently scarcely advanced his positions, which meant that his career was less than brilliant. By then his posts were really sinecures for an artist, which suited the poet and painter who spent an increasing amount of time in his newly acquired estate at Wang River. There he made an art of friendship; there he wrote and painted. His sorrows were now personal—the loss or the death of a friend, the death of his mother. For these years his public office was secondary.

We may pause a moment in his career to consider Wang Wei in the light of his great contemporaries Li Bai and Du Fu, who during most of this period experienced more violent upheavals. We have suggested how Wang Wei was affected by his external conditions. Bitterness and depression show through the poems recording his first banishment. We will find something analogous, at least briefly, during the terrible period of An Lushan, when he was imprisoned by one side, released, worked unwillingly for the rebels, and then was imprisoned again by the newly restored emperor's son. These events also affected his poetry. But his drama was not as constant as that of Li Bai and Du Fu, who only much later in their lives attained situations of relative tranquility, permitting a certain serenity and resignation to enter their poetry.

Li Bai was dismissed from the court, though he apparently scoffed at his dismissal. He was often reputed to be something of a wild man, "the spirit of freedom walking in a bloody land" (Payne, p. 158). Like Du Fu he spent much of his life wandering, and he walked away from situations of favor. As for Du Fu, he failed the imperial examinations on two occasions, and during the An Lushan Rebellion he suffered such poverty that one of his sons died of starvation.

Can we link life and poem reasonably enough to say that Du Fu was nurtured by so much failure and perceived so much injustice that he found himself writing poems with a distinctly engaged, social core? Du

Fu's social observations are of a stark, even brutal nature when describing the tyrannical prime minister, Yang Guozhong, brother of the emperor's consort, Yang Guifei.

> Behind the red painted doors wine and meat are stinking:
> On the wild roads lie corpses of people frozen to death.
> A breadth of hair divides wealth and utter poverty.
> This strange contrast fills me with unappeasable anguish.
>
> (Payne, p. 186)

By clear contrast, Wang Wei's observations on injustice remained largely of an immediately personal nature—his compassion for a friend who failed the dreadful imperial examination, sympathy for a woman separated from her love, anger and sympathy for a woman forced to give up her husband to become an unwilling concubine for the emperor. His criticism tends to be gentle and subtle or even wistful, however, as when he comments with intimate resignation and weary bitterness on his own life as an unwilling bureaucrat.

Cult of Friendship

In his years of wandering during his first exile, Wang Wei cultivated one of the oldest and foremost arts in China—friendship. In the court he had not only professional friendships but true attachments, and this comes out with particular feeling when a friend falls into disgrace or is dismissed. The open secret of Wang Wei's poems is the unifying emotion of friendship. It is the common cord that goes through court and country experiences; it is the consolation and joy of his seclusion in the mountains; it becomes the sorrow of distance during his banishment. In life he was shaken profoundly by the death of his wife and later of his mother. After the latter's death in 750, Wang Wei withdrew into solitude at Wang River for two, possibly three, years of mourning. But there are no extant love poems to his wife or formulas of affection to his mother. Friendship occupied the entire stage of both everyday feelings and deepest passions.

In this cult of friendship, Wang Wei is very Chinese. Although there are unsurpassed love poets in Chinese (a fact that gives discomfort to some apologists for Chinese moderation and constraint)—including Li Shangyin (812?–858) and the wondrously poignant women poets, Yu Xuanzhi (ca. 843–868) and Li Qingzhao (1084?–ca. 1151)—the expression of love is normally secondary to a pronouncement of friendship. Even in Li Bai, known for a life with three wives and many passionate loves, friendship prevails. Although in Ezra Pound's eyes Li Bai may have been a passionate love poet who died drunk, embracing the moon in the Yellow River, it is rather his tender poems to the younger friend, Du Fu, that touch us most and persist. In Wang Wei we observe friendship in all of its scope.

To be cut off from a friend is ordinary grief. To write a personal poem to a professional who has fallen, in favor or through death, is a very special genre. The greatest example in the English language is Walt Whitman's "When Lilacs Last in the Dooryard Bloomed," his poem to the assassinated Lincoln. In Greek we hear a poem attributed to Plato lamenting the death of his friend Dion and distinguishing, as did Wang Wei, between the station of the public man and his personal feeling for him:

> *Inscription for the Tomb of Dion, Tyrant of Syracuse*[4]
>
> Tears were fated for Hekabe and Ilium's women
>   from the day of their birth,
> but Dion, just when you triumphed with famous works,
> all your wandering hopes were cast down by the gods.
> Now dead in your spacious city, you are honored
>   by patriots—
> But I was one who loved you, O Dion!   (Bamstone, 1988, p. 182)

When Wang Wei's friend and protector of the literati, Zhang Jiuling, was sent off in disgrace, Wang wrote a poem that, if known at the time, could only have harmed him in the palace warfares. Zhang was prime minister, an excellent poet who had lost out in a battle with his opponent, Li Linfu. Zhang was banished to the countryside—familiar words?—and we hear Wang Wei's own wishful ambiguity as he too imagines himself in a pastoral setting. Like Plato's poem, Wang Wei's ends with a declaration of the special nature of his affection.

> *For Zhang, Exiled in Jinzhou, Once*
> *Minister to the Emperor*
>
> Where are you? I think only of you.
> Dejected I gaze at the Jingmen mountains.
> Now no one recognizes you
> but I still remember how you helped me.
> I too will work as a farmer,
> planting, growing old in my hilly garden.
> I see wild geese fading into the south.
> Which one can take you my words?

Wang Wei's poetry conveys every major shade of friendship, with perhaps the exception of outrage at friendship's betrayal. Curiously, betrayed friendship is a theme undeveloped in Chinese poetry. Closer to the Chinese spirit is Wang Wei's gentle yet poignant quatrain "A Farewell in the Mountains," conveying universal notions of friendship's persistence, with all of its insinuations of seasons, loss, and rebirth.

> I've just sent you off in the mountains
> and the dying sun closes my wooden door.
> When green again lives in spring grass,
> O my friend, will you too come back?

In these lines and elsewhere, Wang Wei relies on the classical practice of pairing statements in couplets in such a way that an event or abstraction in the first line is metaphorically paralleled by an observation of nature in the second. Sometimes the order is reversed as here in the second couplet in translation. Wang has just sent his friend off into the mountains. The consequence? The finality of the dying sun closes his wooden door. But nature will be reborn; green will live again in the grass. Will the friend also live again in his presence?

A friend who will not live again is the poet Meng Haoran, for whom Wang writes an elegaic quatrain. Meng Haoran was a disciple of a Zen Buddhist master and one in the school of poets associated with Wang Wei. An old catalog of Wang Wei's paintings includes a portrait of his friend Meng Haoran. Early in life Meng was a hermit. He emerged from seclusion to try his luck at the court. If the legend has any truth to it, he apparently failed miserably in an encounter with the emperor, who earlier had viewed him with esteem. Meng was sent home to Caizhou, an island in the Han River, where soon after he died. When Wang Wei went south to conduct examinations, he visited the grave of the older poet, Meng Haoran.

Weeping for Meng Haoran

> I look for my old friend. He is nowhere.
> Only the Han River flowing daily into the east.
> I might ask for the old man of Xiangyang
> but among mountains and rivers his Caizhou island
>   is today desolate.

The poem is a quest for the meaning of his friend's death, who now is nowhere. The river flows, time flows, but not the life time of his friend. In the second parallel line of the couplet, we see the analogue in nature. The third line asks disarmingly where the old man of Xiangyang might be. Here Wang Wei resorts to allusions. In addition to the old man who was his friend, there are at least three other famous old men who anciently lived on or who visited Meng's island. A network of allusions in earlier poems, including ones by Meng, takes us back to a pair of friends, two famous generals—Qai Mao, who once lived on the island, and Qao Qao, who visited him there. Finally, there was another well-known figure, the hermit Pang Degong, who lived there too. To a Chinese reader the import of these allusions is that although the island is desolate and empty today it will always be associated with worthy figures, now including his friend Meng Haoran. In some strange, perhaps sophistic, but just way, his hope is fulfilled and confirmed through the many books containing annotations of Wang Wei's elegy, including this book of translations. In his sonnets Shakespeare tells us more than once and with no little pride the Horacian commonplace that his love will live through his verse. When Wang says, "I might ask for the old man of Xiangyang," he appears to console himself and his deceased friend with the notion of immortality through art and the memory of reputation. But in the very next line he catches himself. The reality of death returns and he points up the loss, the desolation, the empty island.

The An Lushan Rebellion

In 755 the An Lushan rebellion took place, changing the empire and Wang Wei's life. Prime Minister Li Linfun had died three years earlier, to be succeeded by Yang Guojong, the weak brother of Emperor Xuanzong's concubine, Yang Guifei. The empire's most illustrious days had passed, and when in 756 the frontier general An Lushan led a large army on Luoyang and Chang'an, in less than a year the twin capitals had fallen. The emperor fled ingloriously to the mountain province of Shu, present-day Sichuan. Wang Wei's role after An Lushan's brief triumph is less clear, and much has been written in judgment of the poet. Some accounts are plausible. He evidently tried to catch up with the fleeing retinue but was caught by the rebels. Thereupon, it is said, he took drugs either to die or to make himself an invalid. An Lushan imprisoned him in the Puti Monastery in Chang'an but later summoned him to the court, where he was given a position in the rebel government.

After the flight to Sichuan, the emperor resigned in favor of his son Suzong, who in late 757 recaptured Chang'an and the empire. Wang Wei was again in trouble, this time for having worked for the rebels, but he was soon pardoned. Two plausible explanations are offered. Wang Wei's younger brother, Wang Jin, who held the high office of vice-president of the ministry of justice, petitioned the emperor to pardon his brother, even asking the emperor to reduce his own position, if necessary, in order to free him. The second explanation concerns poems Wang Wei wrote after his capture. When he was in prison under An Lushan, he had heard of a tragic, humiliating event. The court musicians were forced to play for the rebels at Frozen Emerald Pond. According to the account in the *Miscellaneous Records of Minghuang*, the musicians played with tears in their eyes. One of the musicians threw his instrument crashing to the ground in protest and was immediately arrested and dismembered before the audience as a lesson. When Wang Wei's close friend, the poet Pei Di, with whom he had collaborated in writing quatrains at his Wang River retreat, managed to see him, Wang secretly dictated two poems to Pei about the incident. Somehow these poems, copied on the back of a sutra by the head abbot, survived and were widely circulated. They were proof of Wang Wei's revulsion against the new conquerors, of an unwilling collaboration, and were said to have persuaded Emperor Suzong to restore him to his former office. The title of Wang's poem, longer than the actual quatrain, tells the story. It is the title and annotation at once, so permitting the author to restrict the four lines of verse to poetry.

> *When I Was a Prisoner in Puti Monastery, Pei Di*
> *Came to Visit. He Told Me How the Rebels Forced the*
> *Court Musicians to Play at Frozen Emerald Pond. They*
> *Sang, and When I Heard This, My Tears Fell. Secretly*
> *I Composed these Verses and Gave them to Pei Di.*
>
> Ten thousand houses with stabbed hearts emit the smoke
>   of desolation.
> When will officials again serve the Son of Heaven
>   in the court?
> The scholar tree's autumn leaves drop on the empty palace.
> At Frozen Emerald Pond, a clamor of pipes and strings.

This is an extraordinary poem, untypical in tone and image for its drama. The startling first line, "Ten thousand houses with stabbed hearts emit the smoke of desolation," has the quasi-surreal expression of violence found in Federico García Lorca's *Romancero gitano*: "A thousand tamborines of crystal / were stabbing the dawn" (García Lorca, pp. 66–67). The parallel line of the couplet is direct as a bullet. It asks, when can we return to the legitimate ruler? The second couplet uses a symbol from nature, the leaves of the scholar tree. They fall on the empty palace, meaning disaster and death have come to the usurped palace. The final line is again direct. It recounts the shrill musical drama enacted under duress, under threat of death and actual murder in the presence of the audience.

Wang Wei's attitude under the rebels remained for centuries a controversy. Some Confucian scholars in the twelfth and thirteenth centuries condemned Wang Wei for collaboration, for not committing suicide, or for not succeeding in his attempt to do so when he took drugs to make himself sick so as not to have to serve under the rebels. Yet at the same time poems and a novel were written romanticizing his actions. By now the moral shadows are gone or in his favor. We like the simple explanation of the late Robert Payne, who suggested that "he cared little enough for either of the contending powers" (Payne, p. 150).

While Wang Wei clearly cared enough for his emperor to keep up an official career, the poems reveal a constant temptation to throw aside everything for seclusion, and in his last years escape and seclusion were more and more the subject of his poems. Everything points to the pragmatism and detachment of the reluctant bureaucrat. He turned increasingly to Buddhism and meditation. If there is any question of his orientation, read one of his many profoundly mysterious yet lucid poems about old age. To read what we suppose to be the late Wang Wei is to enter a labyrinth of clarity.

About Old Age, in Answer to a Poem by Zhang Shaofu

In old age I ask for peace
and don't care about things of this world.
I've found no good way to live
and brood about getting lost in my old forests.
The wind blowing in the pines loosens my belt,
the mountain moon is my lamp while I tinkle
    my lute. You ask,
how do you succeed or fail in life?
A fisherman's song is deep in the river.

The narrator rejects things of the world, knowing he has found no good way of managing his life back at the court. Instead, he lets nature's wind loosen his belt, he plays his instrument, he hears the fisherman's song in the river. He asks for little and everything. What is the meaning of the song? His peace, his knowledge is *not* to know and certainly not to tell. As Jorge Luis Borges leads us to the precipice or to the second of death, or out or into dream in search of the one true word without ever, of course, pronouncing that impossible word, Wang Wei also carries us simply, through nature and art, to the poem's closure, which he leaves unclosed so that we can hear.

Not much is known about the last four years of the poet's life other than what the poems suggest. We do have a list of the posts, with dates, that he held at Chang'an. He received four promotions, including a return to his original advisory position, before the rebellion, of grand secretary of the imperial chancellery. His last post was his highest, in reality a sinecure, a kind of assistant secretary of state. Yet personal ambition and external drama were gone. We can suppose that the poet found his real life in his villa at Lantian (Blue Field Mountains) on the Wang River, visiting friends, wandering in the mountains.[5] In fact there is now an even more decisive contrast between court poems, which speak of aging, lament for youth, and weariness with the institution of the palace, and mountain poems, where he is happy, loving the Tao, and lost to time. His high positions have little meaning to him, and we hear not merely the expectations and worries of an unwilling official but a deep plaint:

Winter Night, Writing about My Emotion

The winter night is cold and endless
as the palace water-clock drums the hour.
Grass is white clouds of heavy frost
and aging trees reveal a bright moon.
Beautiful robes frame my wasted face.
A red lamp shines on my white hair.
Now the Han emperor respects only the young.
I look in my mirror, ashamed to go to court.

Here we see Wang Wei through a cold winter night that is bright with the moon caught in the branches of decaying trees. He is also in the winter of his life, listening to the endless drumming of the palace water-clock, his wasted face, like the cratered moon, floating above his beautiful robes. He looks in his mirror, which may be the moon, and is ashamed to go to the court where the emperor respects only the young.

The full routine of his day is seen in the next lines. Wang Wei never shouts nor proclaims despair. Rather, he is concisely factual. In the following poem he records his life as in a confessional diary. At the same time the lines are resonant with symbols—the shadow of the plum trees, a random bell, birds, a jade pendant swaying, discarded court robes. This mere listing, unfleshed out, conveys the atmosphere of self-consciousness and pain in the poem, which he leaves understated, with chaste artistry.

For Official Guo to Whom I Relate My Routine

Sun and haze quiver on arched gates and high pavilions.
Willow catkins float in the shadow of plum trees.
With night a random bell pierces the courtyards
    of the Forbidden City
    and officials' homes.
Most of these clerks are gone, yet birds sing.
At daybreak with my jade pendant swaying
I drag my body up to the Gold Palace.
In the evening I hand in documents I wrote out
    for the Son of Heaven.
I strain to follow him, but I am old.
Soon I'll lie down sick and put off my court garment.

The anxiety and weariness of the city are gone when the poet is in the company of mountains, clouds, the Tao, and perhaps an old woodcutter. He is happy. In the court there is the constant measuring of office, age, influence, class. But in the hills, when he meets a peasant, he talks, clearly without reference to class, in one of his best-known poems on seclusion and with precise mystical implication.

My Cottage at Deep South Mountain

In my middle years I love the Tao
and by Deep South Mountain I make my home.
When happy I go alone into the mountains.
Only I understand this joy.
I walk until the water ends, and sit
waiting for the hour when clouds rise.
If I happen to meet an old woodcutter,
I chat with him, laughing and lost to time.

He chats and laughs, forgets to go home, forgets time, whether worldly time of age, or time of the Tao where time is not measured spatially like clock time but exists in its own unmeasured space.

Wang Wei does not articulate his thoughts or the borders of his meditation with theological words. As in virtually all of his poetry the conceptual is suggested by specific images, and a translation of the object into an abstraction does not, in his eyes, bring one closer to truth. The thing itself has as much validity as an idea to which it leads in a Buddhist or Platonic heaven. Yip Wai Lim writes that Wang Wei comes closer than Wallace Stevens does to achieving Stevens's ideal of striving for the object rather than its abstraction, expressed in his title "Not Ideas about the Thing but the Thing Itself." Yip is absolute in his declaration: "Wang Wei is Phenomenon itself: no trace of conceptualization" (Yip, p. vii).

Wang's language is largely free of abstraction. His way to the conceptual is through the particular, through the object in nature, which inevitably has a strong symbolic meaning. In the tradition of other great religious poets, Hanshan, Gerard Manley Hopkins, Saint John of the Cross, he remains, in image and word, relentlessly a poet of things, whatever the burden of hermeneutics or ideology a reader may find in or wish to impose on his work.

When Wang Wei was near death, according to the biography in the *Old Tang History*, he asked for his brush, wrote farewell letters to his brother Jin and to friends asking them to receive the Buddha's teachings, put down his brush, and died. He was buried on his estate at Lantian, next to his mother, near Chingyuan, the Buddhist monastery he had earlier petitioned the emperor to establish in her honor. According to one account, perhaps legendary, on Wang Wei's death the emperor asked his younger brother Wang Jin to gather all of his poems to present to the throne. Jin did so, among friends and relatives, coming up with the present collection of some four hundred poems. Jin claimed that because of the events of the years 742–755, only "one out of ten of Wang Wei's hundreds and thousands" of poems survived. Of the 400 extant pieces, 371 are attributed today to Wang Wei, and some of these are exchange poems with poet friends, such as the Wang River sequence of 40 poems, half of which are by Pei Di. Compared to Sappho (who is known largely through fragments), or Christopher Smart (whose savaged work survived mutilated from his awful last years), or numerous classical Chinese poets who sometimes are no more than a name, or Wang Wei's own paintings, which survive only by reputation and in a few dubious imitations, much of Wang's poetry has survived. History has been generous in the preservation of the music of a silence.

The Music of a Silence

Silence is a major note in the special music of Wang Wei's poetry. Like any musical notation, its resonance and meaning are determined by the surrounding notes. So in one context the stillness is peace, a peace in nature that is audible because the stillness is clarified by external sounds.

Few people see the acacia blossoms fall,
night is quiet, the spring mountain empty.
The sudden moon alarms mountain birds.
Long moment of song in the spring ravine.
                              ("Birds Sing in the Ravine")

When we hear a bell in the deep mountain or overhear birds singing in a ravine, the "long moment of song in the spring ravine" drops sound into a void and so by contrast evokes the dominant mode of silence. In lengthening the duration of the moment of sound, even the adjective *long* provokes awareness that the song is intruding in a norm of quiet. In these instances we are dealing with sound and silence that are physical and measurable.

A second silence, an extension of the first, is the usual metaphorical meaning of silence in Wang Wei. Silence in nature as in the mind occurs when the mountains are empty, when the mind is empty, when the external phenomena of the world or the distracting earthly mind and body have all been silenced. Then the speaker in the poem escapes from the normal self and is free to move to another dimension of awareness. We see the process begun, when through the exercise of reading scriptures, the monks are released from the noise of peaks:

Before the forest dawns they read Sanskrit.
Their nightly meditation quiets the peaks.
                    ("Stone Gate Temple in the Blue Field Mountains")

Wang Wei initiates his own removal from the "tangled net of the world" and from his faltering mind, writing,

My love for the tainted world weakens daily
as the stillness of meditation eases my mind.
                              ("The Stillness of Meditation")

Through this silence one undertakes the ecstatic journey to a goal of release, exultation, union. As Mircea Eliade describes the Taoist mystical experience, one returns to the beginnings of all things; free from time and space, "the spirit recovers the eternal present that transcends both life and death" (Eliade, p. 31). The Taoist journey is a return to a lost transcendental state as to a Paradise or a Hesiodic Golden Age. If we use a Western Plotinian or Judeo-Christian translation of the mystical experience, from the dark night of obliteration one moves from darkness into illumination and *unio mystica*. In the East the first two steps are similar, purgation of the self and illumination, from which, in the third step, one passes into union with the Tao or the attainment of nirvana. Although the terminological translation of the mystical experience differs (because each theology programs transcendent experience with differing linguistic intentionalities), the experience, whatever its interpretation, is essentially the same (Barnstone, 1983, p. 20).

In Wang Wei, then, the first instance of silence is *physical*. It is the *silence of the outer world*. The outer world is quiet, a precondition for the second silence, which is *spiritual*. It is the *silence of the mind*, purged of distracting phenomena in preparation for the mystical act. So the metaphor of silence moves us from the physical to the spiritual, from worldly senses to their annihilation in favor of the eye of the spirit. The third silence in Wang Wei involves the *silence of the mystical meditation* itself, when thought stops, words halt, and we move through light toward absolute stillness. From physical and spiritual nothing, from the Spanish *nada*, Kabalistic *ayin*, Taoist *wu*, Indian *sunyata*, we move to the absence of words, to a lexical void, to the experience itself, beyond these differing terms for nothingness that charter the theologies of the world's religions.

In summary, we have three silences of (1) the outer world, (2) the cleansed mind, (3) the mystical experience. When ordinary language is silenced, we move beyond words to the ineffable. Yet the problem for Wang Wei as a poet is precisely how to express these silences in language. His special solution, as we shall see, is his coded language of nature.

Although we say we are beyond language, the poet—the mystic as well as the scholar reporting mystical experience—uses language to describe this act, uses words, including the word *silence* itself. Because it is established that ordinary language will not do to describe the "indescribable," another tongue is invented, which we may call the language of indirection. With the failure of conceptual language come the experience and oblique allegories of the mystic. The philosopher Ludwig Wittgenstein concludes the *Tractatus* with a most mysterious aphoristic declaration on the limits of language: "What we cannot speak about we must consign to silence." Yet Wang Wei, whose life was the pursuit of silences, was, of course, not content to assign his experience to silence. Silence was both discipline he subjected himself to and the subject matter of his poetry.

This third and ultimate silence in Wang Wei is the ecstasy of stillness. Stillness signifies that there is neither sound nor movement and no obtrusive dualities. We no longer know, nor reason, nor describe. We move from verbal to substantive being (or substantive *nonbeing* in Taoist and

Buddhist terms). We are the experience. The need to go beyond language (and, by extension, the self) is common to all metaphysical systems whose goal is transcendence. Wang Wei's preferred Taoist author, Zhuangzi, has many anecdotes that reveal the inadequacy of words. Words are like fish-traps to catch fish. Once the fish is caught, forget the trap (Watson, 1971, p. 302). And to Laozi, the legendary father of Taoism, we have the aphoristic declaration, "He who knows does not speak; he who speaks does not know." In the West, Saint John of the Cross's "negative way," the *via negativa*, requires the expulsion of language, as it does of all ordinary knowledge:

> for I remained unknowing,
> rising beyond all knowledge.   (John of the Cross, pp. 58–59)[6]

Similarly, the Buddha was suspicious of language and knowledge and would not limit himself by engaging in cosmological and philosophical speculations. His method, by choice, was oral transmission of ideas— Socrates had the same objection to freezing meaning in language—and even the Buddha's oral speculations were minimal. Words go so far but do not take us to nirvana. Words fail because the absolute is inexpressible. In a famous instance the Buddha remained silent, refusing to answer fourteen questions concerning the *avyakata*, the inexpressibles. He would not become doctrinaire—the doctrinaire Buddhist sects came later and perhaps rose as very distinctive sects because of the Buddha's unwillingness to make pronouncements.

But the Buddha did—like John of the Cross in his allegories, Jesus in the parables, Kafka in the nightmares—offer stories. A secret is not compromised by analogy, and the word of truth, which traditionally must never be uttered, which loses truth if spoken, remains unsaid. When Wang Wei seeks "the oblique way," he will speak of seeing "white clouds and the empty mountain," a paradigm of his way of speaking on both a literal and metaphorical level at once. He depicts the landscape for itself and his Buddhist purposes. Thus, the frequent "empty mountain" also evokes the empty mind, the meditation state or the moment of Chan awakening.

The Buddha tells the story of the man who was struck by a poison arrow. He would not allow the surgeon to remove the arrow until he knew every detail about the man who struck him, about the arrow and the string. The man died because he insisted on knowing. So the Buddha refused to discuss philosophical matters with words. Only in wordless silence do we know what is of another order of knowing. The Buddha explained his insistence on silence and refusal to succumb to language: "Because it is not useful, because it is not connected with the holy and spiritual life and does not contribute to disgust with the world, to detachment, to cessation of desire, to tranquility, to profound penetration, to illumination, to Nirvana!" (Eliade, p. 93).

Yet how do we come to that silence, which is the access to nirvana or to some process we call transcendental? Even the Buddha has had to tell us a story to prove the inadequacy of language and the benefit of silence. As we know, Wang Wei uses the parable of nature for his entry into silence, into meditation. Like the Buddha, like John of the Cross, like Rumi and all of the mystics, he has his oblique language to circumvent the limitations of conceptual language. Consider the ending of "Message for a Monk at Chongfan Monastery":

> A cottage over the valley, a window facing the hills,
>   soundless and barren.
> Who could know there are human affairs in the valley?
> From the town when you look out
> you see only empty clouds and the mountains.

By now we can decode the familiar clues. In this poem of typical quiet clarity, of exquisite simplicity, the voice is personal and intimate. The familiar elements of nature bring one, through silence, to the moment of meditation.

Taoism and Chan Buddhism

In the introduction to *Hiding the Universe: Poems by Wang Wei*, Yip Wailim speaks of the Taoist *quietism* in Wang Wei and enunciates the depth of stillness in the poems: "The state of stillness, silence or quiescence is ubiquitous in all Wang Wei's poems. He is the quietest poet in Chinese and perhaps in all literary history. The 'voices' one hears in his poetry are those one hears in absolute silence" (Yip, p. x). In Taoism the contemplation of nonbeing, of nothingness (*wu*) occurs through the vehicle of silence. And silent contemplation of the *wu* is the Taoist bridge to silent Buddhist contemplation leading to nirvana.

Wang Wei's references to the Tao and to Buddhism are about equal in number. Taoism, native to China, provides a greater source in regard to allusions to specific Taoist sages and the works of Laozi and especially Zhuangzi (Chuang-tzu). Certain qualities that pervade Wang Wei's poems—simplicity, spontaneity, tranquility, the harmony of self and universe and of the phenomenal world and nonbeing, the Yang Yin symbolism of polarity and alternation to convey strength and weakness, things and illusion, worldly noise and mystical silence—all point to his Taoist orientation. The poems in which he refers openly to Buddhism tend to be less literary, perhaps less natural, but more religiously learned, since Buddhism developed in India as a systematic theology. He is specific in his Buddhist terminology, using the Chinese equivalents for dharma, meditation, nonrebirth, nirvana. Although Wang Wei was never doctrinaire and offered no close theological ordering of thought, whatever tendency to method he revealed is distinctly Buddhist.

Wang Wei's formal religious training was as a Chan (Zen) Buddhist, and as earlier mentioned, he studied ten years with a Chan master, Daoguang. Chan was the principal version of Mahayana (Greater Vehicle) Buddhism, which came from India to China and was also the closest to Taoism. Chan focuses on the concrete things here in this world, in our time and space. But these finite measurements also dwell in the infinite, and so one moves naturally, in alternation, between this-worldly and otherworldly, between a perception of nature and mystical deliverance. To move from the concrete to the abstract was their method. It is not surprising that a poet like Gary Snyder, imbued with Zen (Japanese for Chan) and the poems of the Buddhist poet Han Shan, whose *Cold Mountain* he translated, should himself write poems whose imagery, although implicitly transcendental, is immaculately concrete.

In regard to the similarities between Taoism and Chan Buddhism, Pauline Yu summarizes:

Those similarities between the two strains of thought which are most frequently noted include: the mystic appreciation of nature; an emphasis on spontaneity and naturalness; an iconoclastic deemphasis on scriptures, rituals, metaphysical speculation, and scholarship; and a preference for a pedagogical method which involves colloquial language, surprise, irrationality, enigma, and silence. Indeed, Chan has been accused of not being Buddhism at all, but rather a Chinese-Taoist reaction to the foreign religion; it has no Indian counterpart.   (Yu, p. 119)

Of course, there are also distinctions between Taoism and Chan Buddhism, some of them decisive. Taoism tends to be amoral, whereas Buddhism is very much concerned with morality. And a distinctly Taoist notion is the theme of laziness, which is heard again and again in Wang Wei's poems. There is almost a pride and joy in relaxing in nature, in Whitmanian "loafing," in inactivity, in the feat of doing absolutely nothing.

Cooling Off

Clear waters drift through the immensity of a tall
    forest.
In front of me a huge river mouth
receives the long wind.
Deep ripples hold white sand
and white fish swimming as in a void.
I sprawl on a big rock,
billows nourishing my humble body.
I gargle with water and wash my feet.
A fisherman pauses out on the surf.
So many fish long for bait. I look
only to the east with its lotus leaves.

In such a poem Wang Wei is moving toward the Tao. While the ill-defined Tao (ill-defined because it is beyond words, ineffable) is related to Buddhist nirvana, there are clearly oppositions in their nature and goals. Zhuangzi describes the Tao (the Way): "Quietness, stillness, emptiness, not-having, inactivity—these are the balancers of Heaven and Earth, the very substance of the Way and its Power" (Waley, 1971, p. 44). The Taoist seeks the unbroken ecstasy of unity, escape from the duality of the real. To cite Zhuangzi again, "To be one thing and not to change, is the climax of stillness. To have nothing in one that resists, is the climax of emptiness. To remain detached from all outside things, is the climax of fineness. To have in oneself no contraries, is the climax of purity (unmixedness)" (Waley, 1971, p. 45).

In contrast to the Tao, the Buddhist has little joy, if much ecstasy, little laziness and much discipline; the Buddhist is not asocial but concerned with good deeds and building up merit for an afterlife—a concern not for the Taoist. Although there is the common goal of detachment from the phenomenal world of change, in Buddhism detachment is an escape from suffering and hunger, certainly not from pleasant inactivity. The ultimate goals, the Tao and nirvana, may coincide—that is, the freedom and changelessness that comes with emancipation and deliverance. But how can we know, since by definition that mystical deliverance from time and space, from life and death, from dualisms, differentiation and polarity, lies in the realm of the ineffable? As in all secular Borgesianisms or religious mythologies, a knowledge of the unutterable, of ineffable oblivion, of silence, can be approached only obliquely through analogy, anecdote, and most clearly by example or through the experience itself. To know the unknown color yellow it is best to see it.

In addition to the many aspects and indications of Wang Wei's particular devotion to Buddhism—meditation, celibacy, study under the Chan master Daoguang, the Buddhist monastery he built to honor his mother, a farewell letter to his brother Jin, an essay in praise of Buddhism, and, his prima facie evidence and contribution, the poems—there is a last aspect of Wang's Buddhism, reflecting his life and work; it is contained in his *name*. We are not referring to his given name, Wang Wei, but to his cognomen, his *zi*, the courtesy name that he himself chose, *Mojie*. When combined with his given name Wei, the syllables produce *Weimojie*, the Chinese transliteration for Vimalakirti, the famous Indian Buddhist and associate of the Buddha.

Vimalakirti was a mundane layman and a transcendent sage and also the main figure in a sutra named for him. He was the perfect model for Wang Wei's dual role of urbane official and contemplative recluse. The *Vimalakirti Sutra* contains a well-known story, which by the Tang had already been frequently translated into Chinese. The sutra records that in answer to a group of bodhisattvas who had asked him to explain the concept of nonduality, Vimalakirti kept silent and said no word at all. Only his silence could explain the "thunderous silence," the "great lion's roar of profound silence" (Wagner, p. 124). We have already spoken of the essential illusory nature of language and its limitations in expressing the truth of nondifferentiation. Here the choice of "nondifferentiation" might have been replaced by nonduality, emancipation, deliverance, mystical transcendence, absolute awakening, enlightenment, peace, nirvana, or any word suggesting the bliss of the ineffable. This extreme lexical vagueness and synonymity proves the validity of Vimalakirti's silence.

There is a further interpretation of Vimalakirti's silence that pertains to Wang Wei's poetry: the ultimate equation of silence with the key Mahayana concept of *sunyata*, emptiness, which in Chinese is *kong*. Among the silences of Wang's poetry, the one most often "heard" resides in the word *kong* (empty), his frequent epithet used with *shan* (mountain). It comes up in "Nobody in sight on the empty mountain" ("Deer Park") or as the motif of his celebrated "Living in the Mountain on an Autumn Night."

> After fresh rain on the empty mountain
> comes evening and the cold of autumn.
> The full moon burns through the pines,

a brook is transparent over the stones.
Bamboo trees crackle as washerwomen go home.
Lotus flowers sway as a fisherman's boat meanders
    down the river.
Though spring grass is dry and brown
a prince is happy in these hills.

In translation we have transposed the first line, which in Chinese begins with the two characters *kong shan*, meaning "empty mountain." So the first line of the text starts with the notion of emptiness, of stillness. This is the key, for we shall see that immediately and until (but not including) the closure each line denotes activity. There is the movement of nature—rain, the seasons, the evening. Then the moon affects the pines, the brook moves, the bamboos crackle, women go home. The verbal dominance continues as lotuses sway, a boat meanders, and even the grass turns dry and brown. A prince (whose name is Sun, or Wangsun, [Prince Sun]) stays happy in these hills. The closure suggests stasis, permanence, nonmovement. Here we have another example where the stillness of sound and movement is conveyed paradoxically by its opposite, by noise and activity.

In this much analyzed poem, we should be able to read the signs: *kong*, emptiness, which is Buddhist *sunyata*, offers the possibility of the stillness necessary for meditation. But apart from the still mountains, nature is, by contrast, active. The prince, however, in those empty mountains is also still. His happiness there remains. Presumably, he—Wang Wei's symbol for himself or us—can also stay in such a setting and move contemplatively into permanence, into the end of duality, to the peace of nondifferentiation. Wang only suggests, here and in many other poems, the meditative journey to stillness, but the signs are undeniable. Without such a possible reading of them, the poems would be prettily descriptive but shallow.

"Magnolia Basin" shows the depth of subtle suggestion that Wang Wei can reach. It is a poem of exceptional quietism, even for Wang Wei:

Magnolia Basin

On branch tips the hibiscus bloom.
The mountains show off red calices.
Nobody. A silent cottage in the valley.
One by one flowers open, then fall.

Here is a familiar tension in Wang Wei: the unmentioned presence of the viewer who records the scene is swallowed up in the quiet emptiness of a pure text of nature. Hibiscus blossoming on the branches turn the mountains red. There is nobody about; a cottage in the valley is silent and abandoned. "One by one flowers open, then fall": this is the only motion in all the mountains. Yet if this is so, then who is here to see it? It is the thought problem of Wallace Stevens's first way of looking at a blackbird:

> Among twenty snowy mountains,
> The only moving thing
> Was the eye of the blackbird.

In his fine discussion of Wang's "Magnolia Basin," François Cheng shows just how pure a text of nature this is, pointing out, through an extended analysis of the first line, elements of concrete poetry in the visual appearance of the characters that mirror their lexical meaning (confirming Pound–Fenellosa and negating James Liu in the debate over whether pictorial radicals actively convey meaning in a Chinese character):

木	末	芙	蓉	花
branch	end	hibiscus		flowers

The line is translated "At the end of the branches, the hibiscus flowers." Even the reader who does not know Chinese can easily become sensitive to the visual aspect of these characters. . . . Viewing these characters in order gives the visual impression of the process of a tree blossoming into flower (first character: a bare tree; second character: something is born at the end of the branches; third character: a bud breaks out, 艹 being the radical of grass or flower; fourth character: the bursting open of the bud; fifth character: a flower in its fullness).   (Cheng, p. 9)

The unmentioned observer of the natural scene is the ubiquitous form of Wang Wei meditating in nature. The poet's absence implies his full merging with nature. Cheng finds that this hidden presence of the poet is also embodied in the characters themselves. He interprets the poem as occurring in a scenario in which the poet has contemplated the tree until he is able to "become of 'one body' with the tree and to perceive from the 'interior' of the tree the experience of its blossoming":

. . . a reader who is familiar with the language will not fail to note in addition, through the ideograms, a subtly hidden idea, that of the man who enters the tree in spirit and who therefore participates in its metamorphosis. The third character (芙) contains the element 夫 'man', which itself contains the element 人 'Man' (*homo*); thus, the tree presented by the first two characters is from this point onward inhabited by the presence of the man. The fourth character (蓉) contains 容 'face' (the bud breaks out into a face), which contains the element 口 'mouth' (this speaks). And finally, the fifth character contains the element 化 'transformation' (man participating in the universal transformation). By an economy of means, and without recourse to external commentary, the poet re-creates, before our eyes, in its successive states, a mystical experience.   (Cheng, pp. 9–10)

A poem that is more direct in its use of symbolism is "Suffering from Heat." At first the poet refers to the metaphorical impact of an unbearable natural world; then he employs the specific abstract terms of Taoist and Buddhist speculation—universe, infinity, enlightenment. In this dramatic poem Wang first addresses the immediate outside world, complaining that the summer heat is so intense that the vegetation is burned up, his clothes are unbearable, and even his bamboo mat is too hot to lie on.

> The red sun bakes earth and heaven
> where fire clouds are shaped like mountains.
> Grass and woods are scorched and wilting.
> The rivers and lakes have all dried up.
> Even my light silk clothes feel heavy
> and dense foliage gives thin shade.
> The bamboo mat is too hot to lie on,
> I dry off, soaking my towel with sweat.

As in Eliot's "The Fire Sermon" in *The Waste Land*, the world is a parched and hellish place where bodily existence is torturous. What can he do? Escape. But there is no immediate physical escape. He is not in the cool mountains or the cool season. He acknowledges that he is a victim of his body, that he is held in by external heat and internal turbulence.

> I think of escaping from the universe
> to be a hermit in a vastness
> where a long wind comes from infinity
> and rivers and seas wash away my turbulence.
> When I see my body holding me here
> I know my heart is not enlightened.
> Abruptly I enter a gate of sweet dew
> where there is a medicine to cool me.

Both Eliot and Wang Wei are drawing on the "Fire Sermon" of the *Maha-Vagga*, in which the fire is the fire of passion, of attachment to the senses and the world seen through the senses (Warren, pp. 351–53). Also as in the "Fire Sermon," Wang Wei conceives an aversion for this world of fire, an aversion that makes his heart seek another path. "And in conceiving this aversion, he becomes divested of passion, and by absence of passion he becomes free" (Warren, p. 353). Eliot ends his version of the

"Fire Sermon" by splicing fragments from St. Augustine's *Confessions* between "The Fire Sermon"'s "burning"s, creating a panreligious call for asceticism:

> Burning burning burning burning
> O Lord Thou pluckest me out
> O Lord Thou pluckest
>
> burning

Wang Wei prays (like Eliot's speaker) to be released from the world: "I think of escaping from the universe / to be a hermit . . . When I see my body holding me here / I know my heart is not enlightened." Then he enters a "gate of sweet dew," which cools the mind and frees him of passion. The gate suggests the Way, but the "sweet dew" refers specifically to the nectar of immortality or nirvana. Upon entering the gate of sweet dew, he finds the cooling medicine or, in a word-by-word literal rendering, the "joy of purity and coolness," which is another Buddhist term for nirvana.

In another poem, "For a Monk from Fufu Mountain I Offer This Poem While We Are Eating Dinner," Wang Wei is not on the way but there. These lines are an extraordinary example of two kinds of poetry that normally are mutually exclusive. We refer to a poem descriptive of a mystical experience and one that is the experience itself. The former tends to use conceptual language; the latter, metaphoric or allegoric language. Such a dichotomy is appropriate when we remember that the closer we are to absolute truth, to the word, the more inadequate language becomes and the more obliquely the experience of truth must be approached—hence, the indirection of the symbolic language of metaphor and allegory. In Wang Wei's poem we have neither a complete external description nor a passage composed, as it were, in the midst of the experience itself (the best examples of the latter may be Saint John of the Cross's "Noche oscura del alma" [Dark Night of the Soul], or "¡Oh llama de amor viva!" [O Flame of Living Love] [John of the Cross, pp. 56–57]). What we do have is a combination of the described experience and the experience itself by means of reflection. Wang Wei delineates his turn to meditation, which he encloses in beautiful images of his everyday reclusive life.

> With age I learn the value of quiet
> and feel apart from crowds. Detachment has come to me.
>
> Expecting a monk from a remote mountain,
> first I sweep out my own shabby rooms.

From peaks wrapped in cloud, he descends
to my overgrown grassy hut.

On straw mats we eat pine nuts
and while incense burns we study the Tao.

As day leaves I light the oil lamp
and at nightfall play the singing stone bells.

Tranquility has brought me happiness,
life is slow and full of leisure.

Why worry deeply about return
when body and world are like empty void?

The poem begins with Wang Wei's declaration that he is now apart from that former life of crowds, presumably the city and the court. Moreover, he knows detachment. In a vegetarian setting he shares pine nuts with the monks. Time passes; he is quiet and happy. There is one last remembrance of that other life, of the possibility of return, but then all that is declared as illusory body and world, an empty void. Left unsaid but clearly implied is the key: since the phenomenal world and body are void, he will enter the true void, seeking nirvana.

La Música Callada of St. John of the Cross

We have referred several times to the ecstasy of stillness. Stillness, the vehicle in which ecstasy occurs, contains the double meaning of silence and motionlessness. Since ecstasy is itself a movement, as defined above, for our purposes stillness in Wang Wei begins with silence and ends with motionlessness. Stillness describes the mystical journey of meditation. Wang's stillness and emptiness have a counterpart in Saint John of the Cross's *música callada* (hushed music) and negative way, and it is fitting to make a few comparisons between Wang Wei, who may be thought of as the most accomplished mystical poet of the East, and John of the Cross, the major mystical poet of the West.

Whereas Wang Wei was a layman, a friend of monks, who was also a devoted Buddhist, John of the Cross (1547–1591) was a Carmelite monk and formally a mystic, who defined the mystical process in four books of extensive prose commentaries. From Wang Wei we have one essay on Buddhism. As poets, each wrote extraordinary poems that invite a possible mystical reading; yet being good poets, they had the poetic wisdom to include theological terms only rarely in the poetry. John of the Cross found his simile for union with God in human erotic love, drawn largely from the figures in the bibilical Song of Songs. Wang Wei found his allegory of mystical contemplation in nature, in the empty mountains.

Saint John of the Cross—in Spanish he is San Juan de la Cruz—proposed the negative way. He is at times called *el doctor de la nada* (the doctor of nothingness). The notion of the *via negativa* was not original to John. It was already elaborated in the early centuries in Pseudo-Dionysius. The mystical way, with its ladders of perfection, also appears in philosophical tracts by, among others, Plotinus and Philo, whose diction, with its similes and invitation to flight, is abstract and largely conceptual (Barnstone, 1981, pp. 719, 724). Saint John of the Cross is the poet, and he uses symbolic images to chart his passage from *via* to *via*. Through the dark night the soul seeks to lose its former self. It loses and gains its person as it moves through the *via purgativa, via iluminativa, via unitiva* (the way of purgation, the way of illumination, the way of union).

> Without a place and with a place
> to rest—living darkly with no ray
> of light—I burn myself away.   (John of the Cross, pp. 82–83) [7]

John of the Cross speaks of his journey as a negative way, a passive night of the soul, where, through *unknowing*, one comes upon a mystical understanding. His basic thought is not essentially distant from Keats's negative capability, Henri Bergson's intuition and duration, nor even the Socratic idea of knowing more because one knows that one knows nothing. All of these notions have one common basis: to see, understand, and create, one must first erase previous notions, habits, and patterns of thinking in order to achieve a tabula rasa, or virginal state; from nothing, or *nada*, or dark night, one is prepared to see, understand, and create; so the act of creation, as in Wang Wei, demands a rejection of the old, of the former person, in order to create a new person.

In John we hear the creation in silence, a silence, like Wang's, defined by natural sounds. In John's "Spiritual Canticle" the bride seeks her love, climbing into the mountains. There she listens to nature's clamor until all is calm in "the music of a silence, / the sounding solitude" (*la música callada, la soledad sonora*).

> My love, the mountains and
> the solitary wooded valleys,
> the unexpected islands,
> the loud sonorous rivers,
> the whistling of the loving winds.

> The night of total calm
> before the rising winds of dawn,
>   the music of a silence,
>   the sounding solitude,
> the supper that renews our love.   (John of the Cross, pp. 46–47)[8]

There is only one verb in these stanzas, in the last explanatory line. The rest is a progression of exclamatory nouns and adjectives. The movement of the first stanza halts in the second as a dynamic stasis takes over, a stillness of silence and motionlessness infused with energy. In the happiest moment of union, the silence is the music.

In Wang Wei we have very many examples of such stillness framed in nature's music and an ascension through contemplation to illumination. By now, after so many illustrations from Wang Wei and these few from Saint John of the Cross, the following lines by Wang Wei should hardly need commentary. The title itself is charged with the implications of the contemplative life: "Visiting the Mountain Courtyard of the Distinguished Monk Tanxing at Enlightenment Monastery." The poem concludes:

> Wild flowers bloom beautifully in clusters,
> a bird's single note quiets the ravine.
> In still night he sits in an empty forest
> feeling the autumn on the pine forest wind.

The first line evokes a sensual nature. The bird's cry evokes the larger silence of the ravine. The third line we have read many times. It is the old man in the mountain, contemplating in silence, in emptiness, *sunyata*. But as always, Wang Wei never goes to the instant of no movement, of utter stillness. He is not a saint. He is much too human. He can come close but is too truthful to assume arrival. So he feels the autumn, the next-to-last season of the year, coming in on the pine wind. There is still some movement toward. There is an element of Antonio Machado's "almost" (*casi*), his "almost evening," and "almost happy." On an afternoon in Tang China at Enlightenment Monastery, it is almost still, but the autumn still moves in the wind. Stasis is sought but not claimed.

Poetics of Impersonality and a Personal Poet

Inevitably, the most sensitive students of Chinese literature repeat certain homilies in regard to Wang Wei's posture before nature. Wang Wei is impassive, part of the whole, one among many, as a human figure is in a painting, like a tree, one among many. Wang Wei himself becomes virtually invisible before nature, or at most, to use a favorite Buddhist unitary analogy noted earlier, the poet is a mirror in which all nature and existence are reflected; or nature is a mirror and he, among other things of existence, is reflected in it. These standard views have a cumulative scholarly validity, but applied to Wang Wei they obscure an obvious reading of his poetry. If one reads Wang Wei without prejudice, he emerges as one of the most personal poets who has ever written poetry.

There are actually three related arguments proffered to prove Wang Wei's passivity and impersonality. They are *linguistic*, *aesthetic*, and *religious*. We have already alluded to the Taoist–Buddhist argument. We will take them up in order, linguistic, aesthetic, and return to the above mentioned slippery, intricate, and most important religious argument. In her critical study and translation of Wang Wei's poems, Pauline Yu suggests an affinity between French Symbolist and Chinese theories (Yu, p. 22). "Wang Wei's work," she writes, "is a fulfillment of several key Symbolist aims" (p. 26). She refers, among other points, to the "Symbolists' reliance on the image or symbol to convey meaning impersonally" (p. 26), and cites Paul Valéry's notions of "the absence of an empirical speaker" and Mallarmé's "formulation of a type of impersonality"; and of course she speaks of Eliot's dictum of "depersonalization" and "escape from personality" in "Tradition and the Individual Talent" (which Eliot was subtle enough to ignore in his own poetry). She does quality her view, noting that Eliot himself said, "Poetry is only poetry so long as it preserves some 'impurity.' . . . The 'impure' subject matter of poetry is the poet himself." Yu further declares Wang Wei's impersonality, bringing in the Taoist–Buddhist argument ("if he draws attention to himself at all, it is generally as one thing among many others"). Finally, she states, "his work represents the clearest example of the impersonality defined here" (pp. 26–28).

Let us take up then the question of linguistics and speaker identification (elements of which we have introduced already with "Luan Family Rapids"). Classical Chinese poetry and, for our scrutiny, poetry of the Tang period have few connectives and lack personal pronouns to accompany verbs. The syntactic phenomenon of not using personal pronouns permits a greater sense of authorial detachment and impersonality. This assertion explains in part how the poetry of the early Tang, immediately preceding Wang Wei, was in fact comparatively impersonal as well as

rhetorically ornamental. The authors exploited the possibilities of ano-
nymity offered by classical grammar to conceal or avoid their personal
identity.

Wang Wei's poems were, in fact, a rejection of this practice of con-
cealment. It is essential to emphasize that classical poetry per se neither
conceals nor promotes an authorial voice. While obviously there is much
latitude in interpreting the speaker in Wang Wei or in any classical poem,
and often multiple interpretations are valid, even intentionally so, none-
theless, a reader (and translator) must still choose the speaker, however
evasive he, she, or they may be in the text. The absence of pronouns does
not predicate authorial impersonality.[9] Such a condition offers neither an
easy means of achieving an impersonal Taoist self/world harmony nor a
Buddhist goal of nondifferentiation. To think that there is truly no im-
plied speaker in a Wang poem, or in virtually any classical Chinese text,
is to reduce the text to verbal actions that have neither author nor object
and that surely border on the meaningless. It is the duty of the reader
to find the most probable pronoun to complete the verb (which in some
cases may be intentionally general, so the impersonal and universal *one*
is appropriate). As earlier remarked, the absent speaker is often bodied
forth through context and tradition. Therefore, without benefit of signi-
fier, the signifier is implied. An attentive reading should reveal a probable
profile whose spirit and personality pervade virtually all the poems.

The aesthetic argument for impersonality entails the tendency of some
Chinese and Japanese poets to use a highly objective visual language
in which is realized the dream of Wallace Stevens and William Carlos
Williams to express everything in things. In early Imagist and later Pro-
jectivist American poetry, which sought to obliterate distances between
author and object, there is sometimes a total concreteness, such as in Amy
Lowell's glittering surfaces, Pound's "Petals on a wet, black bough" or
Williams's "A Red Wheel Barrow."

Chinese poetry does contain, then, the possibility of total objectivity
and impersonality through the use of concrete images. It is possible to
conceal personality in concrete objectivity. Wang Wei's poetry, however,
which is insistently concrete—many critics say it has the clearest images
in the Chinese language—is at the same time highly personal, even can-
didly confessional. Precisely the nature of the speaker's intimate identity,
along with the clarity of its images, has made classical Chinese poetry
so attractive to many leading American poets, for whom it has been a
comfortable model and influence. William Carlos Williams, Ezra Pound,

Robert Bly, Gary Snyder, James Wright, and others have imitated its colloquial personal speech, which, in the original Chinese, is adroitly concealed in patterns of euphonic parallel tones and form, a grammatical structure of seeming, but not actual, impersonality.

There is an essential twist to the question of impersonality when we consider the role of the self in Wang Wei's most mystical passages. For here the self, the normal self, does by intention disappear. In keeping with mystical experiences recorded in Western and Eastern sources, as Wang Wei moves into a contemplative mode, he strives to remove himself from things of this world, from the empty mountain, from the body, from ordinary senses. In other words, he leaves behind the self, the person he was. There is therefore a suppression of personality, of the former one; but as he moves into the new condition of ecstatic contemplation, the person suppressed is replaced by another person: the awakened purified self who will be absorbed into the universe or pass into the deliverance of nirvana. There is a loss of motivation based on self, an aim for a kind of impersonality in one's thoughts and actions; but even this impersonality is illusory, for there is really no loss of self but a substitution of one self for another, a transformation of one person into another. The "impersonality" is a linguistic rather than a real notion, for here impersonality refers simply to a changing of names and to that more significant instant of change, the dark bridge, from one personality to another.

The transformation takes place in stillness. By definition, as one moves from one condition of being to another, from one knowledge to another, one moves in ecstasy from ordinary self to an extraordinary extended self that in the West is ultimately deified through union with a godhead and in the East is absorbed into a Buddhist awakening. This absorption in Chan Buddhism is not a cessation of being, is not, as in Indian versions of Mahayana Buddhism, a salvation found elsewhere, but a different level of awareness in this life. In Chan one becomes a Buddha in this very body and awakes and lives with a pure mind, not defiled by dust or hunger, here on this earth.

As for the complete suppression of the self that Yu and others find in Wang's poetry (which we have designated as a transformed self), that could occur only at the moment when the spiritual self is indeed absorbed into the Tao or the deliverance of Nirvana. While Wang Wei speaks of and aspires to detachment and the loss of self, he remains a conflictive soul, with worldly ties subverting the ultimate detachment that would have made him a better Buddhist but perhaps a less effective poet. Moreover, the Taoist element in Chan Buddhism itself conspired with Wang's whimsical, lazy, conflictive, and humorous personality in the midst of his turn to meditation. A few poems, as we have shown earlier, may have total objectivity, and many function as Zen *koans*; yet the argument that Wang's poems reveal no self, no cumulative personal voice, defies both the surface and deep readings of the poems.

Impersonality, *no*, but escape from self—at least in the terms we have suggested—a tentative *yes*, insofar as he wishes to leave one self for another. One of those selves is the desiring self, and Wang Wei's poetry is a lifelong desire to be without desire. The pathos of the poet desiring to be a recluse but compelled, perhaps tempted, to be a bureaucrat, infuses the poetry with its particular emotion. In another poem, "Written in the Mountains in Early Autumn," which in its range and beauty is one one of the strongest and most complete, Wang begins with self-denigrating overheard comments on his ill-conceived, futile court life.

> *Written in the Mountains in Early Autumn*
> I'm talentless and dare not inflict myself on this
>   bright reign.
> Perhaps I'll go to the East River and mend my old fence.
> I don't blame Shang Ping for marrying off his children early;
> rather, I think Master Tao Yuan Ming left office too late.
> With a cricket's cry autumn abruptly falls
>   on my thatched hall.
> The thin haze of evening is saddened with the whine
>   of cicadas.
> No one calls. My cane gate is desolate.
> Alone in the empty forest, I have an appointment
>   with white clouds.

After hearing the crickets of autumn, he recognizes his loneliness, for there is no human voice now, no one calls. The crickets' natural sound points up the empty silence within him. Momentarily he is desolate. In this fierce ambiguity, found in so many poems, we are uncertain how to witness the darkness and promise, the desolate gate and empty forest on the one hand and the white clouds on the other. Although the sad loneliness and emptiness are not necessarily pleasant, they are often the necessary dark bridge, the Western black night of aridity, the solitary purging transition to meditation.

In this poem, rather than the dark bridge, Wang awaits the more cheerful image of white clouds, his most frequent symbol for ascension into and absorption by the light of salvation. He is not there in the clouds, but he does inform us that he sees a Way. In fact, he has an appointment with white clouds, which all his life he has sought to keep.

Perhaps by the very act of recording these poems, Wang Wei invites us, his readers, to join his appointment with solitude. In the splendid poem "Escaping with the Hermit Zhang Yin," he characterizes his bookworm friend with almost impish hyperbole.

> A hermit, he reads endlessly.
> Whenever he soaks his brush with ink he surpasses
> > the sage of grass calligraphy.
> When he writes a poem it makes a classical verse seem
> > like a throwaway.
> Behind closed doors under Two Chamber Mountains,
> he's been a hermit for more than ten years.
> He looks like a wild man
> pausing with fishermen.
> Autumn wind brings desolation.
> Five Willows seem taller as their leaves drop.
> Seeing all this I hope to leave the peopled world.
> Across the water in my small cottage
> at year's end I take your hand.

His friend, so isolated, looks like a wild man of the mountain. As the poem ends, "you and I," of course, refers to Wang Wei and his friend Zhang Yin. However, as he takes Zhang's hand, the poem has shifted to bring the reader into the conspiracy. Suddenly, by the cunning quiet and artful ease of his verse, we observe that Wang has vacillated once more. He prefers a friend to the commitment of absolute solitude. He wants "to leave the peopled world"; yet as he looks out, he sees his friend who is like him, who reads sutras, who turns to the emptiness of nature to try to find the way—who tries, and, of course, humanly, never arrives. There is a uniqueness in knowing that in life one sets out to escape and go beyond life but also that to remain human and alive means not to arrive—and even negates the possibility of complete escape and arrival elsewhere. Like Whitman who (as in the demotic conclusion of "Song of Myself") always seeks more than himself, just when Wang Wei seeks to go beyond himself into nothingness he must yield to his lifelong temptation and embrace fellowship. That knowledge of human journey also confirms that we exist now; specifically, it confirms our ultimate humanity through friendship as he seeks ultimate redemption:

Seeing all this I hope to leave the peopled world.
Across the water in my small cottage
at the year's end I take your hand.
You and I, we are the only ones alive.

The uniqueness of their shared knowledge he shares with us, having confided it to a poem. We overhear the speakers and are inevitably there too, lucky to be there, the only ones alive in the forest.

WANG WEI IN CHINA AND OUR TRANSLATION

In May and June 1972 I was in China as "a friend of the Chinese people," the epithet we privileged visitors in blinders were given then. The nation was screaming through its Great Cultural Revolution. The terror in Tibet, in the cities, in the countryside, and in prisons was all secret, not the privilege of guests to see. Slogans proudly filled the air, together with the unembarrassed demand for "politically correct thought"; there were "mind correction camps" and an atmosphere of intolerance and conformity that even today has not entirely disappeared from the bureaus in China or elsewhere in the world. But poetry then was everywhere: on billboards, on the walls of public buildings, above the tables on the walls of every dining room where we ate, in museums inscribed micrographically on peach pits and observed through a loupe, and in little green or red books translated into enthusiastic Chinglish that were found everywhere on table tops for the benefit of foreign friends from all continents.

The thirty-seven poems in these little books were good, written in traditional verse forms not in the "modern" style, but curiously they all carried the same author's name: Mao Zedong. And he alone was allowed to "fill in" the classical *lushi* and *zi* forms. His poems were studied in daily group sessions by workers, farmers, and "responsible citizens," and there were few Chinese we met who did not know them all by heart. In bookstores in each city I visited they were on sale, but there were no other poets, classical or modern, to be found. Wang Wei had absolutely no meaning between 1966 and 1976. He was exiled from existence. There were eight permitted films during the Cultural Revolution (and versions of them as opera, ballet, and children's plays) and only five book authors in the canon: Marx, Engels, Lenin, Stalin, and Mao. While I was in Beijing, the main bookstores carried only a few government periodicals and works by these authors, including the compendious volumes of its one Chinese writer. When I asked for Li Po, Tu Fu, or Wang Wei, I was told that they were temporarily out of stock.

In those pioneer days there was some literary debate in the periodicals about the relative virtues of Li Po versus Tu Fu, and Du (Tu Fu) came out as cleaner. But neither of these "feudal" poets was popularly available, and certainly not Wang Wei, a Buddhist nature poet. Had the Tang poets been printed in classical characters (which were no longer learned) rather than in the simplified ones, few younger people would have been able to decipher them. Those days of proclaimed nationalism were a denial of things Chinese. Chinese civilization was a stain. There was no place for Wang Wei's retreats, for his hermetic escape into a spiritual countryside, for his ecstasy of stillness.

When I returned to China in 1984 with my son Tony, Wang Wei had surfaced. A country had vanished and reappeared as a distinct totality. In comparison with those exultant days of the Cultural Revolution, the nation had become, despite snooping by neighborhood informants and a thousand related ills, a precinct of unimaginable freedoms. We both taught at Beijing Foreign Studies University. I was a Fulbright professor and we were relatively independent citizens, employed by the government and provided with cards, badges, and housing allowance. As teachers, we could travel virtually anywhere, including the villages of Gobi Turkistan and Tibet, where we went unguided and without supervision. True, in Beijing we were still kept protected from the people, safe behind the walls and patrolled gates of the huge Friendship Hotel, which our Chinese friends called "our cosy prison." But it was a thrilling year to be in China, one of extraordinary change and liberalization, a good moment that we all thought would endure and improve. It came between the ideological cycles of the antipornography and antibourgeois liberalization campaigns. Bookstores were filled with volumes of all kinds, Chinese and foreign, from the ancient *Shijing* poems and Han dynasty songs to Kafka's *Castle*; even the works of the underground Democracy

Movement and "Misty School" poets could be obtained in samizdat. The Tang and Song poets were in the good stores.

Among my friends, colleagues, and students, I was surprised at how Wang Wei was so often the preferred poet in the Chinese language. In the marvelous trinity of Tu Fu, Li Po, and Wang Wei, Wang's philosophy and aesthetic were taken as the enlightened way. As once they knew Mao's verses by rote, now older professors and younger poets recited Wang with the sentiment of discovering a memory that had been forcibly concealed. Wang Wei was the enduring China. Even his dissident loneliness was a political statement just as the act of being a filmmaker, novelist, poet, or painter carried with it the possibility of important dissent and artistic statement. The industry of the modern creative artists was concordant with the remembrance of the recently maligned and banned classical authors.

Tony and I translated Wang together, as well as a small book by Mang Ke, an excellent underground poet, who was courageously central in the 1979 Democracy Movement days. Like others, he was fired from his work and jailed because of his publications. Tony was also attentive to other younger writers, working with them to translate and put together a representative collection entitled *Out of the Howling Storm*. Guided by our Buddhist nature poet, who was at the center of our Chinese experience, we found our rooms filled with young and older Chinese poets. Our activities quickly became known in a city where the real information is not official but word of mouth. We in turn spent many evenings in the Beijing hutongs where our poet friends lived—some of the coldest and happiest evenings of my life.

Since the early fifties, when I was a graduate student at the School of Oriental and African Studies in London and beheld Arthur Waley arriving daily in formal English dress (except for his bicycle clips, which he did not remove from his trousers while at school), I had a passion for Chinese poetry. My interest in Greek and Spanish poetry, its cousins in the West, only enhanced the Chinese side. These three poetries expressed every state of the soul through landscape images, each human event and discourse through word pictures. The Chinese character as a semiotic sign is the ultimate phonic icon. The Spanish poets in whom there is most clearly an equation of soul and landscape imagery (and I use *soul* only as a useful, secular verbal sign) were Saint John of the Cross and Antonio Machado. Saint John (1547–1591) is the poet of spirit whose speech is immaculate nature and love; Antonio Machado (1875–1939), by affinity the most naturally Chinese poet of the West, is a quiet Wang Wei of the Castilian and Andalusian landscape, whose lonely meditations as he walks through his mountains bring him, laughing, into Wang Wei's own wooded hills.

Given these good circumstances, it was natural that Tony—already a skilled poet, craftsman, and linguist—and I should have turned to Wang Wei's poems as our project for the year in China. Wang Wei is the quietly profound and complexly plain poet of China—and also a legendary Tang painter. He is among the handful of the world's poets. So we dedicated two marathon nights a week to working on his poems with Xu Haixin, then my student at the university, and other evenings to reviewing and polishing what we had done in draft. I don't wish to say more than a few words about our notions of translation—which are evident, I hope, in these English versions—particularly in these days of satiety after having just finished an overly big book on translation history, theory, and practice. Without moving into questions of fidelity, license, naturalization, imitation, collaboration, reproduction of forms, and the translator as scribe, God, or erroneous slob, I wish only to remember, as a measure, a few words from John Frederick Nims: "The greatest infidelity is to pass off a bad poem in English as representing a good one in another language."

Our method, if not our theory, has been very simple. Wang Wei has a limited lexicon in Chinese in comparison with his contemporaries, and he uses it in infinitely supple ways to make each line fresh and sensitive. We went over each line, character by character. When a character was unknown to us, sometimes we struggled with Xu not to give us interpretations but only ruthlessly dictionary-literal meanings. Xu did the annotations immediately after the first draft of each poem, which was helpful in every way. With all this material, we sought the poetry lines in English.

We finished a version in China that we offered to the Foreign Language Press. We continued work on the manuscript in America for several years, since Xu Haixin was by now ensconced in his own Friendship Hotel at Cornell University. I worked for a few days with Xu in Boston and Bloomington, and Tony and I have revised poems and introductory material in many cities here and appropriately on an island in the Cyclades, which is our Deep South Mountain.

It is good to have one joined voice of son and father. It has been our double happiness. We have been children in our love for Wang Wei, brothers in our shared labor, one, we think, in voice and spirit. A few years ago Moyen Bell, Ltd. put out an admirable book in which some seventeen poets translated the same quatrain by Wang Wei. Here is one more essay in that mysterious and confusingly metaphysical work of presenting a poem to a reader, who will receive it somewhere between Wang Wei's brush and our electronic print. The voice should be Wang's, though now he sings in English. And each poem should add to the cumulative strength, complexity, and shape of that voice; yet, for it to come through as a poem, the reader must also be willing to allow questions of identity and translation process to blur into oblivon so the voice can be heard. If Wang were alive and read American English, I hope he—as we hope you—might make an appointment with white clouds and read these poems of soul, earth, and clouds with pleasure, as Wang's poems, as poems in English. And yes, as poems.

W.B.

TRANSLATION : THE ART OF POSSIBILITY

Many collaborations have made the poems in this book possible. Each poem represents the joining of two Barnstones and one Xu into a translator's trinity, trying among us to incarnate that old ghost, Wang Wei. Each time you hear the voice of Wang Wei in this book you also hear echoes of those poets in English who first came up with equivalents for Chinese poetic techniques. And finally, in your act of reading and rereading, as your mind becomes the final page upon which the poem is written, you complete the poem by allowing its language to speak in your language, by allowing your mind to be inhabited for a short time by the strong friendships, the pristine encounters with nature, and the private revelations of a mind of some twelve centuries ago.

We've tried to be transparent water, to let the poems be seen through us unobstructed, as clearly as stones in a shallow brook, but inevitably, in translation, the poem suffers a sea-change into an other, a doppelgänger. We had to invent a new diction, to limit articles and pronouns in our English in order to retain our sense of the charged particularity of each Chinese character. No padding. Nothing inessential. We have tried to come up with a language as profoundly evocative as the Chinese character while retaining the understated quality of Wang Wei's meditative verse. Robert Hass has said that one of the primary movements of Modernism is away from a Romantic poetry of declaration toward an East-derived poetics of implication. Consider these lines from "Living in the Mountain on an Autumn Night":

> The full moon burns through the pines.
> A brook transparent over the stones.

To learn how to render Wang Wei's lines we went to school, like so many translators of Chinese poetry, in the poetry of Ezra Pound:

> The apparition of these faces in the crowd;
> Petals on a wet, black bough.　　　　("At a Station of the Metro")

Although the moon is round like the stones, and the pines are transparent like the brook, we resisted the temptation of metaphor or simile and simply let the lines work in sequence as parataxis. Similarly, in Pound, it's not that the faces are petals, nor that the faces are like petals, but that the faces are presented to us, the petals are given to us, and the reader takes it from there.

At the same time, it would be disingenuous to say that translation is not interpretation. Before translating, one must learn to read well; it is the secret of life and death in translation. Like Mary Shelley's Promethean doctor, the translator does an autopsy on the poem to see what made it tick, sews its parts together with pieces stolen from other poetic graves, and tries to charge it back to life. Yet we don't wish to usurp the poem through translation as a White House "spin doctor" might usurp the truth of an event. The act of translation, like the act of contemplation of nature in Wang's poetry, is a process of meditation on the riddle of small recorded events: sun slanting deep into a wood, a mountain so far away it dissolves into cloud, reeds trembling in a slight breeze. Sometimes Wang's poems would so possess us that they would blaze immediately into an English poem. Other times we spent days puzzling over a simple quatrain, coming back to it again and again, trying to feel the poem behind the poem that would make these words live.

W. S. Merwin has said that "we look, but we also see. We listen, but we also hear." We needed to look past the characters to see to the poem, to listen carefully to hear the poem. When the poem came, it was with the revelation of moon breaking through the trees. Our most difficult task then was to reencode the enigma—and the possibility of revelation—into the English poem. If the poem, sunk for centuries on the sea-bottom of language, surfaces in a different tongue and century, this sea-change will be into something as strange and as wonderful as its old life. The translator's art is possibility—not prescribing to the reader, but opening the poem to discovery. In this act translators achieve their greatest fidelity.

T.B.

A HERMIT IN THE MOUNTAINS

My Cottage at Deep South Mountain

In my middle years I love the Tao
and by Deep South Mountain I make my home.
When happy I go alone into the mountains.
Only I understand this joy.
I walk until the water ends, and sit
waiting for the hour when clouds rise.
If I happen to meet an old woodcutter,
I chat with him, laughing and lost to time.

Written in the Mountains in Early Autumn

I'm talentless and dare not inflict myself on this
   bright reign.
Perhaps I'll go to the East River and mend my old fence.
I don't blame Shang Ping for marrying off his children early;
rather, I think Master Tao Yuanming left office too late.
With a cricket's cry autumn abruptly falls
   on my thatched hall.
The thin haze of evening is saddened with the whine
   of cicadas.
No one calls. My cane gate is desolate.
Alone in the empty forest, I have an appointment
   with white clouds.

Deep South Mountain

Taiyi Mountain is close to the capital
and its peaks tumble down to the sea.
White clouds come together as I look back
but when I enter blue mist it vanishes.
From the middle peak I see other wild fields,
a valley of shadows, another of sun.
Needing to lodge some place among people,
I shout across a brook to a woodcutter.

In the Mountains

White stones glow in Chaste Tree River.
With the cold sky, red leaves thin out.
No rain on the mountain path
yet greenness drips on my clothes.

Sketching Things

Slender clouds. On the pavilion a small rain.
Noon, but I'm too lazy to open the far cloister.
I sit looking at moss so green
my clothes are soaked with color.

Living in the Mountain on an Autumn Night

After fresh rain on the empty mountain
comes evening and the cold of autumn.
The full moon burns through the pines.
A brook transparent over the stones.
Bamboo trees crackle as washerwomen go home
and lotus flowers sway as a fisherman's boat slips
    downriver.
Though the fresh smell of grass is gone,
a prince is happy in these hills.

Climbing the City Tower North of the River

Wells and alleys lead me to the rocky hills.
From a traveler's pavilion up in clouds and haze
I watch the sun fall—far from this high city—
into blue mountains mirrored by distant water.
Fire on the shore where a lonely boat is anchored.
Fishermen and evening birds go home.
Dusk comes to the silent expanse of heaven and earth
and my heart is calm like this wide river.

**From Dasan Pass, Going Through Shaggy Forests and Dense
Bamboo, Climbing Paths Winding for Forty or Fifty Miles to
Yellow Ox Peak Where I See Yellow Flower River Shining**

A soaring endlessly curving path,
every few miles we have to rest.
I look around for my friends.
They've vanished in the wooded hills.
Rain floods the pine trees
and flows hushed among the rocks.
There are silent words deep in hill water,
a long whistle over the summits.
When I look at South Mountain
the sun floats white through the mist.
A blue marsh is luminous and clear.
Green trees are heavy shadows, drifting.
When I am tired of being closed in,
suddenly a clearing and I'm at peace.

Written in My Garden in the Spring

Green pigeons of spring coo on the roof.
The white apricots bloom by the village.
I chop the high branches of mulberries
and with a hoe dig out water veins.
Migrating swallows know their old home
and people after winter watch a new calendar.
Grieving for someone too far from home
I raise a glass but cannot drink.

Autumn Night Sitting Alone, Thinking Of My Brother-in-Law Cui

Quiet night. All creatures are sleeping.
Interminable sound of cicadas.
In the courtyard a scholar tree creaks in north wind.
Now days and nights are deep in autumn.
I know you're smoothing your feathers
and are about to fly off into the clouds.
Soon my head will be entirely white
and I think only of living by the river.
Since any day or night you'll soar into the heavens,
why say you'll join me in the fields?

Going to the Country in the Spring

Walking on willow tree roads by a river dappled
    with peach blossoms,
I look for spring light, but am everywhere lost.
Birds fly up and scatter floating catkins.
A ponderous wave of flowers sags the branches.

Drifting on the Lake

Autumn is crisp and the firmament far,
especially far from where people live.
I look at cranes on the sand
and am immersed in joy when I see mountains beyond
    the clouds.
Dusk inks the crystal ripples.
Leisurely the white moon comes out.
Tonight I am with my oar, alone, and can do
    everything,
yet waver, not willing to return.

Lodging at Master Dao Yi's Mountain Chamber

An old man perches on White Mountain,
living among clouds and smoke and peaks.

Down below, Sanskrit prayer floods the valley.
It's raining. Petals cover the mountain.

The monk is concealed, his heart without desire,
but his name survives in his teachings.

Birds visit him, return speaking Buddhist law.
Guests depart with the habit of meditation.

All day I walk paths among the blue pines.
At twilight I seek lodging in a chamber

in the cave hidden deep in bamboos,
and hear waters plashing in the transparent dusk.

Sitting on my mat and pillow I am involved
in rose clouds of the sunset.

Am I merely a transient guest?
I will serve Buddhism until I cease.

Stone Gate Temple in the Blue Field Mountains

Creeks and summits are brilliant at sunset.
I laze in a boat, my way in the wind's hands.

Watching wild landscapes I forget distance
and come to the water's edge.

Gazing at lovely far woods and clouds
I guess I've lost my way.

How could I know this lucid stream
would turn, leading me into mountains?

I abandon my boat, pick up a light staff
and come upon something wonderful,

four or five old monks in contemplation,
enjoying the shade of pines and cypresses.

Before the forest dawns they read Sanskrit.
Their nightly meditation quiets the peaks.

Here even shepherd boys know the Tao.
Woodcutters bring in worldly news.

They sleep at night in the woods
with incense, on mats clean as jade.

Their robes are steeped in valley fragrances;
the stone cliffs shine under a mountain moon.

I fear I will lose this refuge forever
so at daybreak I fix it in my mind.

People of Peach Tree Spring, goodbye.
I'll be back when flowers turn red.

From Ascetic Wang Wei to Hungry Zhang Yin

You like to set traps for rabbits and hares
and dangle a hook for the darting scales of fish.

You stuff your mouth and belly.
Is that your notion of loving a hermitage?

My nature is to be clean and quiet.
I eat only vegetables to be free of dust and passions,

yet you are unrestrained, even lavish,
as you gorge food from a caldron.

In my house at the foot of South Mountain
I grow still and lose my body.

I walk among birds—they don't scurry,
and among beasts I am with friends.

Bonfire sunset and clouds are my companions.
The hazy whiteness is my clothing.

I am like Zhen, a true ascetic;
why ask me to be your hermit brother?

Inspired by the Mountains Around Us I Write
For Brother Cui Jizhong of Puyang

Autumn inspires us. We feel happy,
resting by the pond
or strolling by West Wood,
surprised by mountains looming near the gate.
Dark colors race for a thousand miles.
Peaks crack through above the clouds.
Sawtooth mountains face the State of Qin,
hiding Jin Pass.
Sun falls, glazing the lingering rain,
and dusky haze witnesses the returning birds.
Old friend, you look just the same
whereas I sigh at my bald head.

Written on a Rainy Autumn Night After Pei Di's Visit

The stuttering blur of crickets quickens.
My light robe is getting heavier.
In freezing candlelight I sit in my high house.
Through autumn rain I hear a random bell.
I use white laws to handle mad elephants
and unearthly words to test old dragons.
Who would bother to visit my weedy path?
Though nothing like the hermits Qiu and Yang,
in my refuge I am lucky and alone.

Cooling Off

Clear waters drift through the immensity of a tall
    forest.
In front of me a huge river mouth
receives the long wind.
Deep ripples hold white sand
and white fish swimming as in a void.
I sprawl on a big rock,
billows nourishing my humble body.
I gargle with water and wash my feet.
A fisherman pauses out on the surf.
So many fish long for bait. I look
only to the east with its lotus leaves.

A Picture of Mountain Life

In quietness I close my firewood gate.
A whitish immensity faces the dropping sun.
In every pine are nesting cranes
yet no one comes by my cottage.
Tender bamboos have new bloom on them.
Red lotuses have shed old clothes.
On the bay, lamps and bonfires shine.
Water chestnut pickers are coming home.

Lazy about Writing Poems

With time I become lazy about writing poems.
Now my only company is old age.
In an earlier life I was a poet, a mistake,
and my former body belonged to a painter.
I can't abandon habits of that life
and sometimes am recognized by people of this world.
My name and pen name speak my former being
but about all this my heart is ignorant.

Writing on a Piece of Shale

A gushing brook. I'm happy sitting with this piece
    of shale
as the willow brushes my wine glass.
If you say spring wind ignores the heart
why does it carry blossoms to me?

East River Moon

The moon, spat from a mountain's broken mouth,
hangs remotely over my firewood gate.

A thousand trees share a hole in the damp sky
but then some black clouds pause overhead.

Sudden moonlight ties unsteady images to whiteness,
in cold dew the earth starts to breathe.

An autumn brook plashes in a still ravine
as blue mist breaks over deep rocks.

Purity flows into my dark dream
while cracked shapes hug the empty peaks.

Standing by my harp-room window over the pine river,
drowsy in the morning, I cannot think.

About Old Age, in Answer to a Poem by Subprefect Zhang

In old age I ask for peace
and don't care about things of this world.
I've found no good way to live
and brood about getting lost in my old forests.
The wind blowing in the pines loosens my belt,
the mountain moon is my lamp while I tinkle
    my lute. You ask,
how do you succeed or fail in life?
A fisherman's song is deep in the river.

Answering the Poem Su Left in My Blue Field Mountain Country House, on Visiting and Finding Me Not Home

I live a plain life in the valley's mouth
where trees circle the deserted village.
I'm sorry you traveled the stone path for nothing
but there is no one in my cottage.
The fishing boats are glued to the frozen lake
and hunting fires burn on the cold plain.
Temple bells grieve slowly and night monkeys
chatter beyond the white clouds.

THE WANG RIVER

SEQUENCE

AND OTHER POEMS

My country estate is at Wang River Ravine, where the scenic spots include Meng Wall Hollow, Huazi Hill, Grainy Apricot Wood Cottage, Deer Park, Magnolia Enclosure, Lakeside Pavilion, Lake Yi, Waves of Willow Trees, Luan Family Rapids, White Pebble Shoal, Magnolia Basin, etc. Pei Di and I spent our leisure writing quatrains about each of these places.

Huazi Hill

Migrating birds are leaving endlessly,
fall colors come to mountain after mountain.
All the way up Huazi hill a sadness,
staining every far boundary, drifts on.

Deer Park

Nobody in sight on the empty mountain
but human voices are heard far off.
Low sun slips deep in the forest
and lights the green hanging moss.

Grainy Apricot Wood Cottage

Its beams are cut from apricot wood,
its roof is woven of fragrant reeds.
I wonder if clouds under the rafters
float into the human world as rain.

Magnolia Enclosure

Autumn mountains drink the sun's last rays.
Floating birds follow their mates.
At this hour colors leap into clarity.
No place for evening mist to dwell.

House Hidden in the Bamboo Grove

Sitting alone in the dark bamboo,
I play my lute and whistle song.
Deep in the wood no one knows
the bright moon is shining on me.

At Lake Yi

A flute drifts beyond the lake.
At dayfall I send my friend off.
On the waters I turn my head:
Green mountains fold up white clouds.

South Hill

A light boat is heading for South Hill.
North Hill faint beyond harsh waters.
Houses and people across the lake,
I see them far, far. We are strangers.

Luan Family Rapids

In the windy hiss of autumn rain
shallow water fumbles over stones.
Waves dance and fall on each other:
a white egret startles up, then drops.

White Pebble Shoal

White Pebble Shoal is clear and shallow.
You can almost grab the green cattail.
Houses east and west of the stream.
Someone washes silk in bright moonlight.

Waves of Willow Trees

Separate rows of silky willows touch,
and reflections merge into clear ripples.
The scene is not like the palace moat
where spring wind aches with departure.

Lakeside Pavilion

A light boat greets the honored guests,
far, far, coming in over the lake.
On a balcony we face bowls of wine
and lotus flowers bloom everywhere.

Magnolia Basin

On branch tips the hibiscus bloom.
The mountains show off red calices.
Nobody. A silent cottage in the valley.
One by one flowers open, then fall.

Meng Wall Hollow

I made my new home at Meng Wall.
Old Trees? Only some rotting willows.
After me, who else will lodge here,
aimlessly grieving for past owners?

Return to Wang River

Bells stir in the mouth of the gorge.
Few fishermen and woodcutters are left.
Far off in the mountains is twilight.
Alone I come back to white clouds.
Weak water chestnut stems can't hold still.
Willow catkins are light and blow about.
To the east is a rice paddy, color of spring grass.
I close the thorn gate, seized by grief.

You Asked about My Life. I Send You, Pei Di, These Lines

A wide icy river floats to far uncertainty.
The autumn rain is eternal in the mist.
You ask me about Deep South Mountain.
My heart knows it is beyond white clouds.

To Pei Di, While We Are Living Lazily at Wang River

The cold mountain turns deep green.
Autumn waters flow slower and slower.
By the lattice gate, I lean on my cane;
we hear cicadas in the wind at dusk.
The failing sun rests on the dock
and lonely smoke rises from the village.
You are as drunk as legendary Jie Yu
madly singing in front of Five Willows.

Living Lazily by the Wang River

Living here at the White Group Retreat,
I'll never return to the city's Green Gate.
Often I lean on a tree brushing the house
and study villages on the distant meadows,
green oats mirrored in river water
and white birds soaring to the mountains.
Lonely Yuling—who turned down a great post—
is merely pailing water for his garden.

Written at Wang River Estate in the Rain

Rainy days in the empty forest. Smoke rises late
as I steam greens and boil millet to take to the paddies.
Above the foggy waterfields fly white egrets
and an oriole sings in dense shade of summer trees.
In the mountain I practice silence, contemplating
    morning hibiscus.
I pick hollyhock beneath a pine, a vegetarian now,
no longer looking for position, an old man living in
    the wilds;
why should seagulls still be wary of me?

Leaving Wang River Estate

I can't bear to set out in my horse and carriage.
In pain, I ride under green creepers hanging
    in the pine grove.
Even if I were calm about leaving blue mountains,
how could I give up these green waters?

Appreciating the Visit of a Few Friends at a Time When I Left My Official Post and Lived in My Wang River Estate

Oh, I am not yet dead,
despairing over this life alone!

Now I live behind the screen of Blue Field Mountains,
bent over, plowing thin land.

At year's end I pay taxes
so my bowls of rice may go for temple sacrifice.

In the morning I go to the waterplots,
dew still on the grass.

At dayfall, seeing the stove smoke,
I go home, balancing my shoulder pole.

Knowing that friends are coming,
I use my foot to clean around the wicker gate.

What do I have in my basket for my friends?
I cut melons, beat the date tree.

Looking up at a crowd of nobles,
I am merely a white-haired old man.

I am ashamed of not having a bamboo mat,
so I cover the ground with twigs and weeds.

In rough waters we climb into a boat
to find lotus flowers.

We study white sturgeon
hovering over white sand.

Tribes of mountain birds float by cliffs.
Sun is covered with vague pink clouds.

Friends enter carriages or mount horses
and suddenly like rain disperse.

Sparrows riot in a deserted village,
roosters crow in empty courtyards,

and I return to loneliness and seclusion,
breathing double hard and sighing.

POEMS WRITTEN AT HUANGFU YUE'S CLOUD VALLEY ESTATE

Birds Sing in the Ravine

Few people see the acacia blossoms fall,
night is quiet, the spring mountain empty.
The sudden moon alarms mountain birds.
Long moment of song in the spring ravine.

Lotus Flower Pier

Every morning I sail out to pick lotus flowers.
The river is long so I often return at dusk.
I don't splash as I pole my boat,
afraid of wetting the flowers' red blouses.

Dike with Cormorants

A cormorant dives into red lotuses
and soars up again over clear water.
Then feathers sleek, a fish in its beak,
it stands erect on a drifting old log.

Duckweed Pond

In spring when the pond is deep, wide,
I watch the light skiff cross to me.
Green duckweed slowly meshes behind;
then willow branches sweep it open.

A RELUCTANT OFFICIAL AT THE EMPEROR'S COURT

To My Cousin Qiu, Military Supply Official

When young I knew only the surface of things
and studied eagerly for fame and power.
I heard tales of marvelous years on horseback
and suffered from being no wiser than others.
Honestly, I didn't rely on empty words;
I tried several official posts.
But to be a clerk—always fearing punishment
for going against the times—is joyless.
In clear winter I see remote mountains
with dark green frozen in drifted snow.
Bright peaks beyond the eastern forest
tell me to abandon this world.
Cousin, like Huilian your taste is pure.
You once talked of living beyond mere dust.
I saw no rush to take your hand and go—
but how the years have thundered away!

On the Way to Morning Audience

White and clean stars float up toward the dawn,
a far misty and gloomy daybreak in the void.
Still dark, the haze around the scholar tree
    persists.
The blather of city crows is just starting
    to die out.
Now I hear the hum of words from the High Palace.
I can't make out the cloak room.
Silver candles form into rows.
Solemnly, carriages pass through the Golden Gate.

Spring Night at Bamboo Pavilion, Presenting a Poem to Subprefect Qian about His Staying for Good in Blue Field Mountains

Night is quiet. All creatures are resting.
Beyond the forest, occasionally a dog barks.
I remember living here in the mountains,
my only neighbors far west of the ravine.
One morning you came here. I envy you.
Back there we have carriages and official hats.
You prefer picking ferns in this unknown place.

On Being Demoted and Sent Away to Qizhou

How easy for a lowly official to offend
and now I'm demoted and must go north.
In my work I sought justice
but the wise emperor disagreed.
I pass houses and roads by the riverside
and villages deep in a sea of clouds.
Even if one day I come back,
white age will have invaded my hair.

For Zhang, Exiled in Jingzhou, Once Advisor to the Emperor

Where are you? I think only of you.
Dejected I gaze at the Jingmen Mountains.
Now no one recognizes you
but I still remember how you helped me.
I too will work as a farmer,
planting, growing old in my hilly garden.
I see wild geese fading into the south.
Which one can take you my words?

Goodbye to Wei, District Magistrate of Fangcheng, on His Way to Remote Chu

I remember the remote water reeds,
a few souls walking in the vast region of Chu,
high geese over the long Huai River,
the ancient city of Ying like a flat wasteland.
From your envoy's carriage you can hear pheasants
    feeding their young
and the small county drum answering the cock.
If you see a local official, don't blame him
if he pulls out his scroll of complaints.

**Seeing Off Prefect Ji Mu as He Leaves Office and Goes
East of the River**

The time of brightness is long gone.
I, too, have been passed over.
It's fate. No complaint colors my face.
The plain life is what I enjoy.
Now that you brush off your sleeves and leave,
poverty will invade the four seas.

Ten thousand miles of pure autumn sky.
Sunset clarifies the empty river.
What pleasure on a crystal night
to rap on the side of the boat and sing
or share the light with fish and birds
leisurely stretched out in the rushes.

No need to lodge in the bright world.
All day let your hair be tangled like reeds.
Be lazy and in the dark about human affairs,
in a remote place, far from the emperor.
You can gather things smaller than you;
in the natural world there are no kings.

I will also leave office and return,
an old farmhand, plowing the fields.

Winter Night, Writing about My Emotion

The winter night is cold and endless
and the palace water–clock drums the hour.
Grass is white clouds of heavy frost
and aging trees reveal a bright moon.
Beautiful robes frame my wasted face.
A red lamp shines on my white hair.
Now the Han emperor respects only the young.
I look in my mirror, ashamed to go to the court.

Written for He the Fourth in Return for a Country Cotton Wrap-Around Hat

In this country hat lies your kindness
and it is better than gold.
It reminds me of seclusion, a bird concealed on a
    branch.
It's right for my heart to abandon officialdom.
In the morning court I put it aside
but in the evening I wash and pin it on.
Then I feel far from dust and noise
as if I were entering the forest with you.

Saying Goodbye to a Friend Returning to the Mountains

Mountain in gray silence. There is no one.
It's hazy blue and very wooded.
Many dragon officials fill the court.
What are you up to in this empty village?
Few understand your essays. Deep thought.
Tao is hard to reach. Act alone.
You're happy with spring floating on rocks.
Ecstatic with pines and your straw cottage.
To climb into clouds and feed chickens there
or mount a summit to catch your calf.
Immortals give you a date big as a watermelon.
Tigers guard you selling apricots, reaping grains.
I'm ashamed about my work and in the way.
I'm old. Why be greedy about wages?
I'll lay aside my seal to follow you
to the hills, wiser than Chan Yin's guesses.

Saying Goodbye to Qiu Wei Who Failed His Exam and Returns East of the Yangzi River

You failed and are deprived. I pity you,
especially with willow branches bringing in spring.
You're penniless now. How can you travel?
At home you'll have some new white hairs.
You can't manage the outer world of Five Lakes
    nor your intimate Three Mile Dwelling.
You wander lonely between them.
Though you are as good as famous Ni, I can't help you.
I'm an official, and ashamed.

**The Emperor Commands a Poem Be Written and Sent to
My Friend, the Prefect Wei Xi**

The abandoned city is utterly desolate.
For thousands of miles the land is empty.
Autumn sun is remote in the towering sky
where returning swan geese are screeching.
The cold pond mirrors the shriveled grass
and phoenix trees drop leaves before tall houses.
The year is about dead.
Observing all this I sing "Old Melancholy Man."
My old friend is not around.
He is far off, east of the forest, alone.

**Saying Goodbye to Ji Mu Qian Who Failed His Exam and
Is Going Home**

When the emperor is a sage there are no hermits.
The brightest come to follow him.
Even hermits concealed in East Mountain
will abandon fern picking.
But when the Emperor's Gate is remote,
don't blame me for going my own way.
You went to the Cold Food Festival at the Yangzi
   and Huai rivers.
You sewed your spring clothes in Chang'an and Luoyang.
Now before this immense road, I lay out drinks
   for us.
My shared heart is leaving.
Soon you'll be floating, pulling a cassia oar,
then brushing through the cane gate of your cottage.
Far trees draw you.
A lonely city blots out the dropping sun.
I abhor what they did.
In what you wrote and are, I am with you.

The Mountain Dwelling of Official Wei

I had to comb the mountain to stumble on your place.
Here I find you alone.
Deep valleys turn with the climbing steps.
Each peak longs to enter your abode.
Your kitchen is lost in a bamboo grove.
You had a silk belt and official seal, now you have
    canes hanging on the opposite summit.
You wear no hat, ride in no carriage but are close
    to nature.
Who says you are sick with incompetence?

Looking into the Distance and Missing My Home at West Building with Official Wu Lang

From the tall building, I gaze at the horizon, thinking.
Eyes reach their limit. Feelings go beyond sight.
My head on a pillow, I see a thousand miles,
glimpsing innumerable houses through the window.
People walk slowly on long roads.
Dim sun in the remote countryside.
My melancholy reaches far beyond the creeks.
Smoke appears, far off and lonely.
You are so talented at writing poems
but I, like a lowly official, just think of going home.
My village can't be seen.
Beyond the clouds is only void.

While I Was a Prisoner in Puti Monastery, Pei Di Came to Visit. He Told Me How the Rebels Forced the Court Musicians to Play at Frozen Emerald Pond. They Sang, and When I Heard This, My Tears Fell. Secretly I Composed These Verses and Gave Them to Pei Di.

Ten thousand houses with stabbed hearts emit the smoke
　　of desolation.
When will officials again serve the Son of Heaven
　　in the court?
The scholar tree's autumn leaves drop on the empty palace.
At Frozen Emerald Pond, a clamor of pipes and strings.

Ding Yu's Farm

Your heart wants to hide away like a bird in a tree
and for a long time you plan escape.
At court we scheme about it.
Now you've given up your seal and are fascinated,
    happy.

Cocks crow in the neighborhood.
Wildlife song follows you.
Farmers are on their way to the fields,
women and girls, already awake, sew white silk.

After opening your chest, folding your clothes,
you shape sentences in unfolded books.
Sometimes you chant tunes about asking hermits
    to visit you
or brush long *fu* poems about idle life.

On a pristine day I gaze at the country;
sun is a mirror on mulberry and scholar trees
    until twilight.
Tree shadows fully clothe the village.
Along the Wei River the woods are dim.

I plod, measure the alleys between huts.
How many wondrous hidden scenes!
I can never forget the Tao. It tells me
how hard to find what my walking about
    discovers here!

I have to leave. I'm cast down. When wildflowers
and aromas return, I'll be back.

Visiting Jia's Chamber on Mount Tai Yi

In my earlier days, perching like a bird and hiding
    out,
I was your neighbor amid sunclouds and haze
and together we drank pineleaf wine
and used napkins made of bamboo skin.
Climbing in the woods we examined every cloud cave.
We picked herb medicines, whether in winter
    or spring.

I belong to the Gate of the Tao
but by mistake was summoned as an official,
a horse to draw the emperor's carriage.
Often I worry that magical pellets and potions are
    prepared
and you will enter the Purple Light earlier than I.

It doesn't take me long to exhaust a thousand ways
    of this universe.
Sadly a hundred new worries assail me.
Your way is harsh and excludes those of us with worldly
    taste.
Often our talents blind us to ordinary truth.
Facing a twin fountain I weep.
When I return to this mountain my host will be gone.

For Wei Mu the Eighteenth

You and I look at each other with the good black
   of our eyes.
We share a white cloud in our hearts.
If we don't go back to East Mountain
grass will take over, daily growing deeper.

For Official Guo to Whom I Relate the Routine of My Life

Sun and haze quiver on arched gates and high pavilions.
Willow catkins float in the shadow of plum trees.
With night a random bell pierces the courtyards
   of the Forbidden City
   and officials' homes.
Most of these clerks are gone, yet birds sing.
At daybreak with my jade pendant swaying
I drag my body up to the Gold Palace.
In the evening I hand in documents I wrote out
   for the Son of Heaven.
I strain to follow him, but I am old.
Soon I'll lie down sick and put off my court garment.

Upon Leaving Monk Wengu of the Mountains and Thoughts to My Younger Brother Jin

I take off my hemp robe and go back to the Court
   of Heaven,
leaving my master to be with the worldly wise.
I've failed not only the man on the mountain
but the moon over the trees.
We used to walk about
and pause at the edge of rose sunset clouds.
Our window opened on the Ying River's north bank;
from our bed we saw flying birds return.
When we ate we were fond of leaning on rocks.
Often we napped by a waterfall.
In good times why go into seclusion?
Yet when the Way prevails the outer world is stilled.
You my younger brother will have a high post
but I will probably take the tonsure.
I sprinkle water and sweep my cane gate.
When you have time, come by and knock.

FRONTIER POEMS

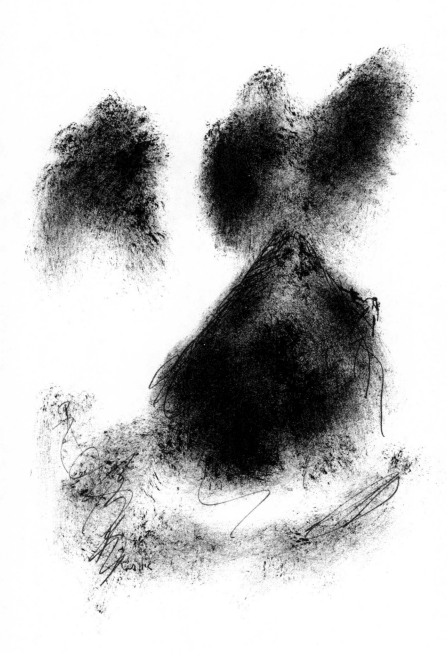

Seeing Yuan Off on His Official Trip to Anxi

Morning rain in Weicheng dampens the dusty ground.
Willow trees give the inn courtyard a fresh greenness.
Why not drink one more bowl of wine?
Beyond Yang Pass there are only strangers.

Saying Goodbye to Ping Danran, Overseer

You don't know the road after Yang Pass.
Only now have you joined the governor of the border lands
where yellow clouds blot out spring colors
and frontier sadness blows from a painted horn.
It takes years to get through the Dry Sea of the Gobi
    Desert
where the Forked River flows on the other side of
    the border post.
When you set out as an envoy to the Tatars be careful:
You may be drinking from a bowl made from the skull
    of the Yuezhi king.

On Long Mountain

Armed with feathered arrows I head for the border,
    blowing a reed flute.
I cross Long Summit.
When clouds yellow, I know the fortress is near.
In white grass I see autumn bleaching the frontier.

Song of Marching with the Army

Horns blow the travelers into movement.
Noisily they get under way with the sad sound
of reed pipes and chaos of neighing horses
as everyone struggles to ford Gold River.
The border sun settles in the desert
while sounds of war rise in smoke and dust.
We'll bind the neck of every chieftain
and bring them as presents for the emperor.

At the Frontier

The Pride of Heaven barbarians are hunting beyond
   the Juyan city wall.
White grass touches the sky and wild fire spreads.
Dusk clouds. Horses gallop the empty desert.
Autumn on the plain is good for shooting vultures.

Morning. The Defending General of Qiang climbs to the
   barbican.
Night. The General Destroyer of Barbarians crosses
   Liao River.
Our Tang emperor, like Han sovereigns, will give jade reins,
   horn-bows
and horses bridled with pearl to a new General Huo.

Watching the Hunt

Strong wind. The horn–bow sings.
The generals are hunting in Wei Cheng.

In withered grass, the falcon's eye is sharper.
In melting snow, horse hooves are light.

They've just passed New Harvest Market
yet are already home at Willow Branch.

They look back. They shot the vulture
in a thousand miles of twilight clouds.

Seeing Prefect Liu Off to Anxi

The road from Yang Pass leads to the world's edge
where there's nothing but smoke of barbarian campfires
   and fortress dust.
In three months of spring, wild geese often fly past.
For endless miles there are few travelers.
Alfalfa follows the Horses of Heaven
and grapes trail the Han envoy home.
We should make those foreign lands tremble.
It's a horror to trade our princesses for peace.

On Being an Envoy to the Frontier

In a single carriage I head for the frontier,
crossing the vassal state of Ju Yan.
Tumbleweed blows around our Han fortress.
Returning wild geese pierce the barbarian sky.
Vast desert. Solitary smoke rises straight.
Long River. The setting sun is round.
At Xiao Pass I meet the patrol. They warn me:
the Grand Marshall is at Swallow Mountain.

The Envoy at Yu Ling

High mountains are cypress and pine forest.
Below, a hill brook stabs a soldier's heart.
The horizons are newborn grass.
The Yellow River flows forever to the east.
At Yellow Dragon Fortress, we warriors worry for our lives.
Will we even recognize the emperor's envoy?

A Tang General Sallies into the Wilderness Beyond Mount Yanzhi to Battle Against the Barbarians

The general came out of heaven, shrewd and brave,
  like an earlier Han hero.
He visits the emperor at Brightlight Palace,
and when leaving, the emperor of the 10,000 chariots
  watches him pass through Twin Turret Gate.
A thousand officials toast him before he goes out
  beyond Five Emperors Tomb.

The general has abandoned his elegant mansion safe inside
  the city's Golden Gate;
He wants to make his body into a Great Wall
  at Jade Fortress.
The fabulous Wei and Huo—who destroyed Tatars—
  might merely serve his cavalry,
and even the General of the Two Advisors was no star
  at court.
What about his own brave warriors from the small kingdoms
  of Zhao, Wei, Yan and Han?
West of the fortress, just hear them shouting!

Once the King of Yue licked dripping gall each day
  to incite his revenge. His men
  already await the bitterness of war.
By drinking wine they're ready to scrape poison
  from their bones if an arrow strikes.

Painted halberds and carved spears chill the white sun.
Banners and huge colorful pennons vanish in white dust.
Remote drums stir waves on the dry sea of the desert.
The confusion of reedpipes shakes the moon over
  Heaven Mountain.

A spectacle! The general in brocade girdles with unicorns,
  belts with hooks from Wu.
Blueblack stallions snort and roans dance.
Grabbing his sword he lops off the arm of the Tatar
  Heaven's Favorite.

Back in his saddle he shares a drink from a Yuezhi bowl—
    one shaped from the skull of a vanquished king.
Each screaming soldier can face a hundred!
The barbarian horsemen look on and weep.

The good general trains his crack troops to go through
    boiling water and fire
but he conquers with his mind, scheming.

Frontier Songs

1

Often I have made the hard trip to Yellow Flower,
but this is my first time at far Fragile Willow Camp.
Each fortress night the broken moon saddens me;
frontier sadness follows like trampled high grass.

2

When very young I left home to be a soldier,
hoping to earn reward with my gold inlaid sword.
Does cold water pierce horses to the bone?
I see only dusk clouds arising at Dragon City.

3

Tatars move outside the far north fortress.
As I draw out my precious sword it sings.
Today as I repay the Emperor's favor,
this morning my own life is nothing.

4

Barbarians near the fortress often attack.
The frontier winds whistle autumn.
All my life ambitious, I welcome fury.
With arrows I fight my way to lordship.

West Long Mountain

He changes horses every ten miles
and every five miles raises his whip.
The general's message arrives:
Tatars have surrounded Wine Spring.
A heavy snow drowns the signal fires.
No smoke on the frontier mountains.

An Old General, on Long Mountain, Complains

Young roaming warriors out of Chang'an
climb a night watchtower to gaze at Mars.
Soon they'll come to Long Mountain Pass. The high moon
    glares.
On the mountain a night traveler plays a flute.
West of the pass an old general despairs.
He stops his horse. Listening, his two eyes flood.
He's been in hundreds of wars and skirmishes.
Generals under his flag are now lords of ten thousand
    houses.
Hair from his yak-tail flag is scattered everywhere to
    the west
    of the North Sea,
but, like ancient Su Wu, he is merely a minister
    of vassal states.

Loss

Clear wind. Bright moon. Loneliness attacks me.
Wanderer in the army over ten years,
you lied to me. When you left you said
you'd write when the wild geese return.

Missing Her Husband on an Autumn Night

I
Ting, ting. Leaking water. Night has no end.
Far far light clouds and a moon wet with dew.
Fall makes hidden insects cry all night long.
I haven't sent your winter clothes; may flying frost
   not come.

2
Cassia shadows begin to cover the moon. More dew.
My silks are thin but I haven't changed my dress.
Far into the night I play a silver harp, eagerly.
My heart is afraid of empty rooms I don't dare
   go into.

DEPARTURES

AND SEPARATIONS

Seeing Zu Off at Qizhou

Only just now we met and laughed
yet here I'm crying to see you off.
In the prayer tent we are broken.
The dead city intensifies our grief.
Coldly the remote mountains are clean.
Dusk comes. The long river races by.
You undo the rope, are already gone.
I stand for a long time, looking.

Seeing Prefect Yang Off to Guozhou

Where are you going, friend?
Baoxie Gorge is too narrow for a carriage.
For a thousand miles it's a path for birds
and gibbons who cry all day and night.
We got drunk at Guanqiao Bridge, offering libations.
   You left.
Now, amid mountain trees you come to Young Woman
   Shrine.
Having parted we share only the same moon.
My friend, listen to the nightjar's song.

Seeing Shen Zifu Off on His Journey Down the River to the East

The dock has many willows but few travelers.
A fisherman rows to the far jagged shore.
My sorrow will haunt you like spring colors
on the north and south banks of the river.

Seeing Off Hesui's Nephew

A boat is coming from the south.
From Jing Gate the vessel will plow upstream.
Beyond misty reeds are clouds in the water
and King Zhao's tomb.
City birds float behind the mast.
The river merges with evening rain, and sadness
    prevails.
It's hard to stand the chattering monkeys
or face cold dank autumn in the Chu mountains.

A Farewell

I dismount from my horse and drink your wine.
I ask where you're going.
You say you are a failure
and want to hibernate at the foot of Deep South Mountain.
Once you're gone no one will ask about you.
There are endless white clouds on the mountain.

Staying Only One Day at Zhengzhou

In the morning I say goodbye to Zhou people.
At dusk I look for a mat to sleep on. Will the Zhengs
    take me in?
I have no friends in this strange land.
A lonely outsider, my friends are a servant and a boy.

The cities Nanyang and Luoyang are invisible
in meadows darkened by autumn rains.
Farmers, fathers of the field, slog home through the weeds.
Shepherd boys let their herds graze in the drizzle.
My host is still out in the paddies.

Around this thatched cottage are seasonal plants.
Insects clamor, merging with loom noise.
Crops ripen amid rioting sparrows.
Last night I was still at Gold Ravine
and tomorrow I'm already off, ferrying across
    the Jing river.
What impels me into wandering
through remote regions for a miserable wage?

Seeing a Friend About to Return to the South

Ten thousand miles all around, the spring heats into
  summer.
Over three great rivers only a few migrating birds
  soar.
The Han River is broadening into heaven.
A lonely guest takes off for Ying.
In Yun young rice grows beautifully.
In Shu the vegetables are fat.
Leaning on the city gate and gazing,
I see my friend's bright coat, far off, vanishing.

Thoughts from a Harbor on the Yellow River

Woman
I live at Meng Ferry by the Yellow River
and my door faces the harbor.
Ships arrive from the south.
Do they carry a letter for me?

Man
You come from my village
and must have news.
When you left, had the cold plum blossomed
by her carved window?

Woman
The cold plums are already in flower
and I hear birdsong again.
I see lush spring grass and despair,
bitterly staring at my jade–clean doorstep.

A Young Lady's Spring Thoughts

Unbearable to watch these endless silk threads
    rain through the sky.
Spring wind pulls them apart and intensifies this
    separation.
Leisurely flowers fall to the green mossy earth.
Only I can know this. No one comes to see me
    all day.

Missing the Loved One

Red beans grow in the south.
In autumn they appear on a few branches.
Pick some.
They wake the solitary heart.

For Zu the Third

Spider webs hang from the beams,
crickets sing near the porch stairs.

At year's end, a cold wind.
Friend, how are you?

My tall house is dead. No one here.
Impossible to tell the feeling when you are gone.

A deserted gate, still and closed for the day.
Only the dropping sun slants into autumn grass.

Do you have a new message for me?
A thousand rivers and summit passes block
    my way to you.

After you left I journeyed to Ru Ying
and last year went back to my old mountain.

We've been friends for twenty years
but never have used our talents.

You're always poor and sickly.
I watch my pennies.

Though it's mid–autumn and we're still not in
    our hermitage
we'll be there by late fall.

Our time together is not these few lost days
    become years
but my missing you is forever.

For Someone Far Away

All year I stay alone in my bedroom
dreaming of Mountain Pass, remembering our separation.
No swallow comes with letters in its claws.
I see only the new moon like the eyebrow of a moth.

Seeing Zhao Heng Off to Japan

I have no way of even reaching a harbor,
so what do I know of worlds east of the sea?

Japan is remote from our Nine States,
leagues away, as far as the sky is vast.

To find your way home, sight on the sun;
a returning sail needs only trade winds.

Dazzling sea turtles darken the sky
and fish emit red waves.

Your home is behind Great Mulberry Trees
and soon you'll be on that solitary island.

You are leaving for a strange realm.
We'll each send word—but will we hear?

Composed on Horseback for my Younger Brother Cui the Ninth on His Departure to the South

You head your horse away from mine at the corner
  of the city wall.
When will we meet again?
There are cassia trees in the mountain.
Don't wait till their blossoms pour like rain.

Morning, Sailing into Xinyang

As my boat sails into Xingze Lake
I am stunned by this glorious city!
A canal meanders by narrow courtyard doors.
Fires and cooking smoke crowd the water.
In these people I see strange customs
and the dialect here is obscure.
In late autumn, fields are abundant.
Morning light. Noise wakes at the city wells.
Fish merchants float on the waves.
Chickens and dogs. Villages on either bank.
I'm heading away from white clouds.
What will become of my solitary sail?

A Farewell in the Mountains

I've just sent you off in the mountains
and the dying sun closes my wooden door.
When green again lives in spring grass,
O my friend, will you too come back?

Red Peonies

Green beauty at ease and tranquil.
Red garments light the shadows.
The pistils almost break with sorrow.
How can spring read the heart?

Weeping for Meng Haoran

I look for my old friend. He is nowhere.
I see only the Han River flowing daily into the east.
I might ask for the old man of Xiangyang
but among rivers and mountains his Caizhou island
    is today desolate.

For Scholar Pei in Fun after Hearing Him Chant a Poem

How bitter the gibbon's wail!
After morning worry comes evening pain.
But O, your song,
please don't imitate the gibbon noise at Wu Gorge.
It would burst the guts of any traveler
drifting unprepared down the autumn river.

Arriving at Ba Gorge in the Morning

Daybreak in late spring, I embark at Ba Gorge,
already missing the emperor's city.
A solitary woman washes in the clear river
as many cocks crow into the morning sun.
Junks form a floating market in this land of waters.
A mountain bridge steps over the treetops.
Climbing high, I see thousands of wells
and two bright rivers far below.
Here people use a strange dialect
but birds repeat the sound of my old home.
The sorrow at leaving my city fades
before the old joy of being in new mountains.

Waiting for Official Qu Guangxi Who Doesn't Show Up

Morning! The city gates have opened.
I arise and listen: confusion of carts.
When I hear the clear sound of pendant jade
I will go out to greet my guest.
A jangle of bells from the imperial garden.
Light rain blows through the spring city.
Though I know perfectly well my guest won't come
I go back inside and await him, eagerly.

For Scholar Xu Who Came to Visit Me and Found Me Away

An official, I've few days in the country.
Few old friends come to my dead-end alley.
Often I must leave in the bamboo sedan.
I'm not snubbing my friends in plain dress.
Have you tasted my homemade porridge?
Why in the world did you dust my cane door?
I wish you had shared a lot of tea with me
and taken my horse for your return.

Sailing at Night beyond Jingkou Dike

A solitary sail floats on endless green water
of this cold lake where dead flowers are falling.
Distant trees come alive with dawn.
When dark comes I overhear Wu songs.
Before me is vagueness of the southern waters
and at my back the North Star touches the clouds
    near my home.
Official duties have torn me away.
My nostalgia is lost in wild flying geese.

Night over the Huai River

Water country. There's no end to the south.
No sure time when my shallow boat will head north.
My feeling for my village is dispersed in waters
    of the Huai.
Here at Ying my dream of return numbs me.
Leaves tumble. I know cold is near.
Mountains stretch with the late sun.
I'm never as calm as in Luoyang. A foreigner,
my vagabond heart is in knots.

Night over the Huai River

As if eternally separated from the world, I lie
   on this hazy water.
It's only a corner deserted by heaven.
In autumn wind leaves drop in the Huai River.
Frozen night. Chu songs moan long.
I spend the night in this wild place. It's not
   China.
Even their perch are inferior to fish in my village.
My solitary boat is weary of floating.
The Yue southlands hide remotely in endless blur.

RICE PADDIES AND POMEGRANATES

Countryside at Qi River

I live secluded on the Qi River.
Deep plains to my east. No mountains.
The river gleams across the village
and sun hides behind mulberry trees.
Young cowherds are walking home.
Hunting dogs follow their masters.
What am I doing, a man in peace?
All day I keep my cane door closed.

Joy in the Countryside

1

Bay wind is sharp on the water chestnut pickers.
Sun west of the village. I lean on my staff.
A fisherman near a mound under an apricot tree
stands there as if at Peach Tree Spring.

2

Spring is green with the lush fragrance of grass
and lofty pine forests cool the summer.
Cows and sheep know their way home.
Official robes mean nothing to children.

3

A remote village below the mountain. Solitary smoke.
High plateau. One lone tree on the sky's edge.
I live in Yan Hui's Half Gourd of Food lane
with the Five Willow Man across the street.

4

Red peach flowers still hold last night's rain
and green willows are caught in spring haze.
Blossoms fall. The houseboy hasn't swept up.
Orioles sing and a mountain guest is sleeping.

5

After drinking wine, I walk by a surging brook.
Holding my lute, it's good to lean on a pine.
In the morning I pick a sunflower in the south garden.
At night I husk grain from the east ravine.

Saying Goodbye to Spring

With each empty day I am older
yet spring comes back each year.
A bowl of wine is the only happiness.
Why grieve over falling blossoms?

A Peasant Family

Last year's grain will soon be gone
but the soft seedlings are not yet up.

In old age we have to eat porridge
and clothes wear out in a year.

Sparrows feed their young on a mossy well
and chickens cackle by the white wicker gate.

A skinny cow pulls a cart made of firewood,
someone in straw shoes drives giant pigs.

Rain pounds down, cracking red pomegranate branches;
in early fall the green taro is swollen.

People sprawl and picnic under mulberry trees,
wander home at night through high weeds.

Living in a place called Valley of Fools,
how can I ask about right or wrong?

Song of Peach Tree Spring

My fishing boat sails the river. I love spring
   in the mountains.
Peach blossoms crowd the river on both banks
   as far as sight.
Sitting in the boat, I look at red trees and forget
   how far I've come.
Drifting to the green river's end, I see no one.

Hidden paths winding into the mountain's mouth.
Suddenly the hills open into a plain
and I see a distant mingling of trees and clouds.
Then coming near I make out houses, bamboo groves
   and flowers
where woodcutters still have names from Han times
and people wear Qin dynasty clothing.
They used to live where I do, at Wuling Spring,
but now they cultivate rice and gardens
   beyond the real world.

Clarity of the moon brings quiet to windows under
   the pines.
Chickens and dogs riot when sun rises out of clouds.
Shocked to see an outsider, the crowd sticks to me,
competing to drag me to their homes and ask
   about their native places.
At daybreak in the alleys they sweep flowers from
   their doorways.
By dusk woodcutters and fishermen return,
   floating in on the waves.

They came here to escape the chaotic world.
Deathless now, they have no hunger to return.
Amid these gorges, what do they know of the world?
In our illusion we see only empty clouds and mountain.
I don't know that paradise is hard to find,
and my heart of dust still longs for home.

Leaving it all, I can't guess how many mountains
   and waters lie behind me,

and am haunted by an obsession to return.
I was sure I could find my way back, the secret paths
   again.
How could I know the mountains and ravines would
   change?
I remember only going deep into the hills.
At times the green river touched cloud forests.
With spring, peach blossom water is everywhere,
but I never find that holy source again.

Things in a Spring Garden

Last night's rain makes me sail in my wooden shoes.
I put on my shabby robe against the spring cold.
As I spade open each plot, white water spreads.
Red peach flowers protrude from the willow trees.
On the lawn I play chess, and by a small wood
dip out water with my pole and pail.
I could take a small deerskin table
and hide in the high grass of sunset.

Peasants on Wei River

Cows and sheep straggle down the deep alley
as afternoon sun slants through the village.
An old man framed in the cane gate
leans on his stick watching for the young cowherd.
Pheasants sing to ears of sprouting wheat
while silkworms sleep by the few mulberry leaves.
Farmers walk home with hoes on their shoulders,
chatting lazily.
I envy this easy life,
and sing the song "Why not return?"

Sharp Landscape after the Storm

After the storm the rice fields expand.
No dust stains the air, and my eye travels
to a small harbor near the city gates,
to trees sloping from village to the river's mouth.
I see white water beyond the bright paddies
and green mountains beyond mountains.
In the busy season no one is loafing.
Whole families are in the fields.

Going Back to Song Mountain

A clear river is like a belt in the abundance of grass and
    bushes.
On the road are few horses and carriages.
The flowing water is full of feelings
but the evening birds fly away, one by one.
A deserted city lies behind an ancient harbor.
All the autumn mountains stand in the setting sun.
At the foot of sprawling Mount Song, the city gate
waits for me to go in. Then closes behind.

Walking into the Liang Countryside

The village has just three houses with old people.
A settlement at the frontier doesn't have neighbors
   on all four sides.
Trees wind-dance by the temple of the field god.
Flutes and drums. People worship the deity:
pouring wine on straw dogs,
burning incense as they bow before a wooden figure.
Holy women circle in a never-stopping dance,
kicking up dust with their silk shoes.

Welcoming the Goddess

Bong! They're pounding drums
at the foot of Fish Mountain.
The bamboo flute hovers in the wind.
Standing by the shore I gaze
at the women priests who begin
to dance in wild shoes.
The banquet table is crammed
with bowls of brilliant wine.
Melancholy wind and night rain.
Are you coming, woman god?
Are you really coming? I'm bitter,
my heart has turned bitter.

Saying Goodbye to the Goddess

Many come to the temple to worship her
and their eyes linger on the jade of her sacrificial
   mat.
When she comes she says nothing and reveals nothing
yet brings rain and evening gloom to empty mountains.
A despondent pipe floats shrieking overhead,
a confusion of funereal strings.
Her chariot is abandoning us.
Clouds evaporate and the rain stops.
How green the mountain is! Waters of the air slowly
   vanish.

For Pei Di, Tenth Brother in His Family

Each day, each night, the vista of wind and shadow is
   grander
while you and I write new poems together.
Quietly we look deep into the far sky,
my cheek resting on a monk's writing board.
Spring winds stir a hundred types of grain.
The orchid grows fragrant by my fence.
Sun warms the small gate of my house
and farmers sing to the spring:
"Pond water, come alive in the paddies
and spread out.
Peach and plum trees are not in flower,
but their branches are heavy with buds.
Get out your walking stick.
Soon our plow will taste the earth."

A White Turtle under a Waterfall

The waterfall on South Mountain hits the rocks,
tosses back its foam with terrifying thunder,
blotting out even face-to-face talk.
Collapsing water and bouncing foam soak blue moss,
old moss so thick
it drowns the spring grass.
Animals are hushed.
Birds fly but don't sing
yet a white turtle plays on the pool's sand floor
   under riotous spray,
sliding about with the torrents.
The people of the land are benevolent.
No angling or net fishing.
The white turtle lives out its life, naturally.

A Visit to Our Village by Governor Zheng of Guozhou

After the rains the grass and groves are fresh
and spring pauses with wondrous glowing sun.
A mirror-grinder stands by the window
while in an orchard someone waters his garden.
A five-horse carriage astonishes our squalid alley!
Children traipse around my old body as I receive our
    guest.
In the kitchen we hurriedly throw together a coarse
    meal.
Forgive us. We are poor as the family of Ran.

Spring Light

Silken willows along the meandering river are lines
 of smoke.
With warm air, water of the cold valley evaporates.
Spring light is like this embroidered path.
Now I hear clear music, stirring even the beautiful clouds.

Spring Outing

A horizon of apricot trees by the river,
with blossoms open in the night wind.
Colors swarm through the orchard
where trees are green waves on fire.

Caught in Rain on a Mountain Walk

Sudden daytime rain fills the air,
a downpour too thick to see through.
In the darkened mountains I feel lightning
and a circling horrendous sea of steam.
Moving across the valley I guess my way through
    floods.
Climbing the mountain, I'm terrified among its clouds.
At night the moon swims over the river in a still
    hazy sky.
Through the mist the song of an oar.

A Drunken Poet

Tao Qian really likes to let it all hang out
and was born mad about wine,
yet from the day he quit his official post
his family has been dead poor
and he can't even cough up a coin for a drink.
What has he got at the Double Nine Festival?
   His hands are empty,
holding nothing but gold flowers.

The poor man is daydreaming for a savior
to bring him booze.
Suddenly an old man in white robes appears
with a pitcher and goblets.
The poet downs bowl after bowl. Why count?

Like a quivering bird he shakes out his cape
and wanders to an empty field,
and roars (to no one at all), "I've nothing left,
   but I'm free!"
His knees wobble. He doesn't know where he is
and drops his palm-bark hat and rain cape into the
   mud,
staggers, pushes on,
singing wildly all the way to Five Willows.
Does Tao Qian make a living? Face his life?
It is improper to ask. He is free.

The Madman of Chu

The madman of Chu looks at you in a stupor
as if his heart were a void.
His hair is barbaric, no hats or belt as he walks
singing down paths in the south fields.
When Confucius tried to talk sense into him
he'd have nothing to do with his benevolence
　　and righteousness.
Secrets of heaven? He didn't care for them,
and why pummel the ground about earthly things?
As for fern pickers, they are stupid,
breaking their backs for a few weeds.

Lady Xi

Even in her favor and extraordinary
place of today
she can't forget her former husband
(whom they forced her to leave.)
We look at her, a flower.
Her eyes flood.
She has nothing to say to the king of Chu.

Song about Xi Shi

Her beauty casts a spell on everyone.
How could Xi Shi stay poor long?
In the morning she was washing clothes in the Yue
    River,
in the evening she was a concubine in the palace
    of Wu.
When she was poor, was she out of the ordinary?
Now rich, she is rare.
Her attendants apply her powders and rouge,
others dress her in silks.
The king favors her and it fans her arrogance.
She can do no wrong.
Of her old friends who washed silks with her,
none share her carriage.
In her village her best friend is ugly. It's
    hopeless
to imitate Lady Xi Shi's cunning frowns.

Lady Ban

There are firefly shadows on your jade window
but no human voice in the gold palace.
Autumn night. You wait on the canopied bed,
    behind gauze curtains.
The lonely lamp persists. It can't go out.

Lady Ban

Lush autumn grass grows around the palace
but your favor with the emperor has withered.
It is unbearable to hear those pipes, those flutes,
as his gold chariot passes your window.

An Old Farmer

The scene is a cottage and an old man
with dangling white hair by a shabby wooden gate.
When the fields are still
he calls in his friends for a drink.
Under his thatched roof, in all the noise,
they are happy, letting off steam.
His short coarse jacket is warm enough
and his sunflower seeds taste good.
If he bothers to talk, it's about his children
      and his grandchildren.
The city market is unknown to him.

The Five Emperors and Three Kings were
from ancient times called Sons of Heaven.
How do you greet someone? With a sword, a spear
or by kowtowing? What's the best way to live?
If you're happy, do whatever you like.
Why despise the old man of the fields?

I'm emptying my camphor trunk. I'm going off
to be easy with my days and live out my remaining
      teeth.

Dancing Woman, Cockfighter Husband, and the Impoverished Sage

The woman from Zhao sings dirty songs
and does dances of Handan
while her husband knocks about, puts on cockfights
for the king of Qi.
With yellow gold he buys songs and laughter from
    a whore.
He never counts his coins.

Xu and Shi, relatives of the Emperor, often come
    to his house.
Their high gates are crowded with four-horse carriages.
A scholar lives in their guest house,
bragging about his rich patron, Zou Lu.
For thirty years his meals are the books he eagerly
    consumes
but his waist belt has no money in it.
His is the way of scholars, of the sage.
All his life he is poor.

A Wealthy Woman of Luoyang

Near me lives the woman of Luoyang, who looks
    only fifteen.
Her husband rides a piebald horse with a jade bridle.
Her maid serves minced carp on gold platters.

Facing each other are many painted chambers
    and crimson towers.
Red peach and green willow trees bend along the eaves.
Gauze curtains shield her as she walks to her carriage
    of seven fragrances.
Precious fans welcome her back to her nine-flower
    canopied bed.

Her bold husband is rich, high-born and young
with more mad pride and extravagance than Ji Lun.
He loves his White Jade, teaches her to dance,
and thinks nothing of showering her with handsome
    corals.

Sun is quenched in the spring window. The lamp of nine
    subtleties flames.
Flakes of nine subtleties drift down like petals.
After entertainment, she forgets to practice music.
She makes up and sits numb in clouds of her own fragrance.

She knows all the rich people in the city
and is always at their homes.
But who pities a girl from Yue, beautiful as jade,
poor and washing silk by the river, alone?

For Taoist Master Jiao in the East Mountains

The master, looking a thousand years old,
has lived on the five holy mountains.
At a glance he tells the age of an old cooking tripod
   (like one the Marquess of Qi owned)
and has just been to Mount Wang Mu where the immortals
   live.
He doesn't care about Confucius and Mohism
yet has endless things to ask a peasant.
When he plays his flute, phoenixes join him.
Can you imagine? He fishes with a shallow brass dish.
He can leap up, float, even speak from the firmament
and his eyes are trained to read in the black of night.

Jiao knows the secret of making immortality pills
and often talks about the first seconds of the universe.

The master finds his calling on dewy blades of grass
as if heaven were lowering a soft-wheeled carriage
   for him.
In quiet mountains the sound of gushing springs
   goes far;
when pines grow high their branches thin out.
Resting on his side, the Taoist martyr asks a woodcutter
what is happening in the human world.

MEDITATING BEYOND WHITE CLOUDS

Sitting Alone on an Autumn Night

Sitting alone I lament my graying temples
in an empty hall before the night's second drum.
Mountain fruit drop in the rain
and grass insects sing under my oil lamp.
White hair, after all, can never change
as yellow gold cannot be created.
If you want to know how to get rid
of age, its sickness, study nonbeing.

Visiting the Temple of Gathered Fragrance

I don't know the Temple of Gathered Fragrance,
lost many miles among cloudy peaks.
In the ancient forest there is no human path.
A bell in the deep mountain. Where is it from?
A brook hiccups through the steep rocks
and sunlight chills the green pines.
In faint twilight where an empty pond curves,
meditation drives out the poisonous dragon.

The Stillness of Meditation

I see as far as Taihang Mountains night and day,
but vacillate and never go there.
You ask me why?
I am tangled in the net of the world.

My younger sister is growing day by day;
my brothers haven't yet chosen wives.
The family's poor, little money comes in,
we save nothing.
Sometimes at the point of flying away,
I look at them and falter.
Sun Deng had his retreat at Long Whistle Tower
among pines and bamboos
but between us is a life's way
and a road jammed with friends and relatives.

My love for the tainted world weakens daily
as the stillness of meditation eases my mind.
Someday soon I'll go.
Why should I wait until the cloud of my age
collapses in twilight?

In a Monk's Room in Spring

The old man likes to read *Lives of the Monks*
and about ways of not eating even a grain.
Soon a mourning dove will be carved on his staff;
four turtles have long supported his bedposts.
Willow trees are fire on the spring mountain,
pear blossoms conceal the evening birds.
Under peach and plum trees near the north window,
the monk sits lazily by his burning incense.

A Summer Day, Visiting Zen Master Cao at Green Dragon Monastery

A man as old as a dragon bell, I walk slowly
to visit a meditation temple,
to ask the meaning of a good heart. Remotely,
I feel the sickness of the void is itself void.
Mountains and rivers are in the Buddha's eye,
the universe in dharma's body.
Don't be surprised that meditation controls hot days
and raises wind over the land.

Visiting the Cloister of Meditation Master Fu

Concealed paths twine through the rocky towering summits.
The dharma temple is lost in clouds and forest.
Feathered beings fly, playing music in the wind.
Heavenly women kneel, burn incense.
Beyond the bamboos, dawn lights half the peaks
but under the creepers water stays cool.
I've wanted to know how to meditate for so long
now I walk a path redolent with spring.

**For Official Yang Who Stayed at Night at Zither Terrace and
in the Morning Climbed to the Pavilion of Storing Books and
Then Quickly Wrote Me a Poem**

You brush the dust away and read sutras on old bamboo
    slips,
waiting for the moon's company to play the singing lute.
In Peach Tree Spring people have never heard a Han name.
Certain pines are Qing Dynasty officials.
Few people return to this empty ravine.
The sunless face of the blue mountain is cold.
I envy you the place where you are perched,
watching a white cloud from far away.

Message for a Monk at Chongfan Monastery

A monk at Chongfan
goes home in the autumn to Mount Fufu, but in spring
 he never comes out again.
A nice confusion of singing birds and dropping blossoms.
A cottage over the valley, a window facing the hills,
 soundless and barren.
Who could know there are human affairs in the valley?
From the town when you look out
you see only empty clouds and the mountains.

To the Host in the Place of the Thousand Pagodas

The Inn is celebrating the festival
and the sailing ship docks.
Your windows border on the Bian River.
The door looks out on passing ships of the Chu People.
A village. Chickens and dogs run about.
Mulberries and elms shade the distant fields.
Few people live here. You are here,
and your pillows and mat smoke with dreams.

Visiting Li Ji

Autumn grass grows in the deserted gateway
where all day long no carts are parked.

Coming to call on you
I enter the deep country lane
and dogs bark in the cold forest.

Your loose hair is still unpinned
and you hold a Taoist book in your hand.

You share my heart, loving the Tao
and pleased with your simple life.

I drink rice wine from Yi Cheng,
and like a hermit of old Luo Yang

I go back to my retreat.

Visiting Old Man Zhao in Jizhou and Having a Meal with Him

Though his place is linked with the outside world,
on closing the door he is a hermit.
If he speaks, he speaks of Chuang Tzu,
and he acts like the sage from Lu, Confucius.
The sun is low and peaceful in the alley
while tall willows are clean over the quiet gate.
With a hoe on his shoulder he's off to weed
    the herb garden;
loose pages of his farm books are drying out
    in the sun.
He moves his writing brush when a guest comes
and cooks wild vegetables in the kitchen.
We both have a fine time getting drunk
and I leave only after sundown.

Green Creek

To find the meadows by Yellow Flower River
you must follow Green Creek
as it turns endlessly in the mountains
in just a hundred miles.
Water bounds noisily over the rocks.
Color softens in the dense pines.
Weeds and waterchestnuts are drifting.
Lucid water mirrors the reeds.
My heart has always been serene and lazy
like peaceful Green Creek.
Why not loaf on a large flat rock,
dangling my fishhook here forever?

Seeing Taoist Fang Off to the Song Mountain Region

Scholarly Fang is leaving.
Flags with yak tail tassels and red pennants lean against
    the stone shrine.
The mountain weighs down to the center of the earth and
    reaches
      halfway up the sky.
A cave drops under the river and opens south of the water.
Pines and cypresses by the waterfall are rained on forever.
With the setting sun green colors suddenly are mist.
I question two white cranes from Needle Mountain.
    Where is Fang?
As happened once to the ancient hermit Su Dan,
the cranes have placed him safely at Nine Dragon Pond.

For a Monk from Fufu Mountain I Offer This Poem While We Are Eating Dinner

With age I learn the value of quiet
and feel apart from crowds. Detachment has come to me.

Expecting a monk from a remote mountain,
first I sweep out my own shabby rooms.

From peaks wrapped in cloud, he descends
to my overgrown grassy hut.

On straw mats we eat pine nuts
and while incense burns we study the Tao.

As day leaves I light the oil lamp
and at nightfall play the singing stone bells.

Tranquility has brought me happiness,
life is slow and full of leisure.

Why worry deeply about return
when body and world are like empty void?

Visiting the Mountain Courtyard of the Distinguished Monk Tanxing at Enlightenment Monastery

He leans into twilight on a bamboo cane,
waiting for me at Tiger Creek.
Hearing tigers roar, he urges me to leave;
then trails a pouring brook back to his cell.
Wild flowers bloom beautifully in clusters,
a bird's single note quiets the ravine.
In still night he sits in an empty forest,
feeling autumn on the pine forest wind.

Visiting Li, a Mountain Man, and Writing This Poem on the Wall of His Home

Everything in this world is like a dream.
When he's madly happy he sings to himself.
I ask his age. Old as a pine tree.
What land does he own? All this bamboo forest.
The herbal medicines he makes, Han Kang sells.
Master Xiang often visits his house.
He hates to lie on pillows and mats
where we can do nothing about white clouds.

**Winter Night, Facing the Snow, Thinking of the
House of the Lay Buddhist Hu**

Cold night drum, its arrow pointing to dawn.
In the clean mirror I see my haggard face.
Outside the window, wind startles the bamboo.
I open the door. Snow covers the whole mountain.
The sky of falling flakes quiets the paths
and the big courtyard is abandoned to whiteness.
I wonder if you are like old Yuan An
in his house, locked away inside, and calm.

**For Zhang Yin, a Friend like a Fifth Younger Brother,
Here Is a Fantasy Poem**

When you were at East Mountain, my brother,
how remote your heart was!
The sun looms but you sleep on.
You eat only when the bells ring noon.
Your hair drapes down your collar;
books are strewn open on your bed.
Your spirit drifts slowly like a clear river.

Often you lie down, facing the empty woods.
Green moss clings to stone,
young grass is soft under pine trees.
Outside your window bird sounds are mild.
By your porch even the tiger is gentle.
A thousand images mean nothing
there in the far Great Void.
You know you are equal to things of the earth
and see the shallowness of being a person.
Before you I suddenly grasp myself.
I don't need to brush hungers away.

In the Mountain Dwelling of Scholar Li

Nobles crowd the steps up to the emperor
but as an ordinary man, Li chooses self-exile.
He follows the alchemist,
making his mountaintop home above the treeline.
No flowers bloom on the back face of the mountain.
Clouds float deep into forests or skim over them.
Already broad daylight, he's still asleep.
Now and then a mountain bird sings long.

Visiting Zen Master Xiao at His Song Mountain Chamber

Heaven is kind to homeless brothers.
The monastery brings sun to the whole mountain.
They eat beneath nesting birds, to the sound of
    singing stones,
and walk in empty forests, their footsteps loud
    on fallen leaves.
A waterfall often drenches the incense table.
In rain, fallen petals soften jagged stones.
Who is in the deep cave under the high pine forest?
Someone holy as an ancient Indian saint.

Autumn Meditation

The balcony's ice wind stirs my thin clothing.
Night. The drum endures. The jade waterclock slows.
The moon sails the Heavenly River, soaking its light.
A magpie breaks from an autumn tree. Many leaves fall.

**With My Friends at the Sutra-Reading Bamboo Garden of Advisor
Shen the Fourteenth Where Young Shoots Abound**

In his retreat the day is quiet and clean.
Tall bamboo is beautiful and slender.
On grown ones are young shoots
sticking through an old fence.
Thin branches have the winged noise of chaos.
A cold moon tumbles into random shadows.
Musicians shape bamboo into dragon pipes,
fishermen cut them into fishing poles.
How can ordinary bamboo compare with green crystal
inside this Gate of the Tao, by altars of eternity?

Moaning about My White Hair

Once I had pink cheeks, now my teeth are black.
Suddenly my white hair is like a boy's pigtail,
    soft and fuzzy.
In one life how many times can the heart break?
If I don't turn to the gate of the void,
how can I purge my heart?

Moaning about My White Hair

How old I am now!
Each day my hair is whiter.
My head nods between heaven and earth.
How much longer can I lodge in the world?
Near my gloomy home a mountain cloud
    circles the meaningless day and night.
A city to the east. Farmlands down south.
I have nothing in common with people today.

Weeping for Ying Yao

How many years can a man possess?
In the end he will be formlessness.
Friend, now you are dead
and thousands of things sadden me.
You didn't see your kind mother into the grave
and your daughter is only ten.
From the vast and bleak countryside
comes the tiny sound of weeping.
Floating clouds turn to dark mist
and flying birds lose their voices.
Travelers are miserable
below the lonely white sun.
I recall when you were alive
you asked me how to learn nonbeing.
If only I'd helped you earlier
you wouldn't have died in ignorance.
All your old friends give elegies
recounting your life.
I know I have failed you,
and weep, returning to my thorn gate.

Weeping for Ying Yao

We send you back to Stone Tower Mountain
    to be buried.
The carriage goes through blue pines and cypresses.
Your bones are buried in white clouds for eternity.
Only mountain waters flow down to the realm
    of the living.

Questioning a Dream

Don't be fooled. Why bother with the shallow joys of favor
    or worry about rejection?
Why flounder in the sea helping others, or being
    abandoned?
Where can you dig up a Yellow Emperor or Confucius
    to consult with?
How do you know your body isn't a dream?

Visiting Official Lu While He Was Entertaining Monks and Writing a Poem Together

Three Virtues are not the same as Seven Graces
but we both look with the dark of our eyes
    on the blue lotus.
Monks beg food only to draw in the fragrance
    of the spirit's incense.
They cut their own garments, patched like patterns
    of rice paddies.
They carry tin staffs to fly through the void.
Some patrons give them gold.
They sit cross-legged in the front porch sun.
Their burning incense licks the bamboo trees.
Cold void. This is the space above the cloud
    of dharma enlightenment.
Autumn color. Five Buddhist heavens of purity
    where the *arhats* live.
Their bodies obey the law of place
but their minds soar in meditation.
They don't mourn the sinking sun
for in them there is a burning lamp.

Suffering from Heat

The red sun bakes earth and heaven
where fire clouds are shaped like mountains.
Grass and woods are scorched and wilting.
The rivers and lakes have all dried up.
Even my light silk clothes feel heavy
and dense foliage gives thin shade.
The bamboo mat is too hot to lie on,
I dry off, soaking my towel with sweat.
I think of escaping from the universe
to be a hermit in a vastness
where a long wind comes from infinity
and rivers and seas wash away my turbulence.
When I see my body holding me here
I know my heart is not enlightened.
Abruptly I enter a gate of sweet dew
where there is a medicine to cool me.

Floating on the Han River

Three waters meet at the Chu frontier.
At Jing Gage nine streams mingle.
Rivers climb beyond earth, beyond the sky.
Mountain colors change between being and nonbeing.
Ahead, regional cities float on the river's shore.
Ripples and waves shiver the far sky.
At Xiangyan, the beauty of the sunlit wind
gets the old Man of the Mountain drunk.

Escaping with the Hermit Zhang Yin

My brother Zhang has five carts of books.
A hermit, he reads endlessly.
Whenever he soaks his brush with ink he surpasses
    the sage of grass calligraphy.
When he writes a poem it makes a classical verse
    seem like a throwaway.
Behind closed doors under Two Chamber Mountains,
he's been a hermit for more than ten years.
He looks like a wild man
pausing with fishermen.
Autumn wind brings desolation.
Five Willows seem taller as their leaves drop.
Seeing all this I hope to leave the peopled world.
Across the water in my small cottage
at year's end I take your hand.
You and I, we are the only ones alive.

NOTES TO

THE INTRODUCTION

1. Antonio Machado writes in "A José Maria Palacio":
  Ya las abejas
libaran del tomillo y el romero.
¿Hay ciruelos en flor?
2. Machado writes in "Galerías," V:
Entre montes de almagre y peñas grises,
el tren devora su rail de acero.
La hilera de brillantes ventanillas
lleva un doble perfil de camafeo,
tras el cristal de plata, repetido . . .
¿Quién ha punzado el corazón del tiempo?
3. In preparing the biographical part of this study, we wish to acknowledge our debt to Marsha L. Wagner's *Wang Wei*. With discrimination and critical insight, Professor Wagner has put together the first general book in English that treats the life and the poems of Wang Wei.
4. The reader should know that the word *tyrant* is not used ironically. In ancient Greek the word *tyrannos* means ruler but not necessarily a despotic or absolute ruler. The tyrant Pittakos of Lesbos, for example, was praised as one of the enlightened "Seven Sages of Greece."
5. In 1984–85 we attempted, with the help of the Writers Union, to visit the remains of Wang Wei's estate at Lantian. We were a few times in Xian, the site of old Chang'an, twenty-five miles from Lantian. We were not able at short notice, however, to get permission from the military command to go there because the estate is now occupied by a military arms factory in the middle of whose courtyard there is a lone tree, which, we were told, was at the center of what was once Wang Wei's estate.
6. Saint John of the Cross writes:
que me quedé no sabiendo,
toda ciencia trascendiendo.

7. Saint John of the Cross writes:
Sin arrimo y con arrimo,
sin luz y a oscuras viviendo,
todo me voy consumiendo.
 8. Saint John of the Cross writes:
 Mi amado, las montañas,
los valles solitarios nemorosos,
 las ínsulas extrañas,
 los ríos sonorosos,
el silbo de los aires amorosos.

 La noche sosegada
en par de los levantes de la aurora,
 la música callada,
 la soledad sonora,
la cena que recrea y enamora.
 9. In summary, classical Chinese poetry does not ordinarily use a character for the personal pronoun. Although the signifier is not employed overtly, the signified is implied through the context. An analogy might be our own lack of a pronoun in English to distinguish between "you singular" and "you plural." In practice, however, the context makes up for the missing signifier, and number is rarely in question and surely is never postulated as the basis for a theory of singularism or pluralism in the English language. Similarly, in Chinese, context and syntax should reveal the intended speaker, even if that speaker is an impersonal general speaker.

N O T E S   T O

T H E   P O E M S

A Hermit in the Mountains

Written in the Mountains in Early Autumn

Line 3. Shang Ping (cognomen Ziping) was a Han Dynasty hermit who was known for his profound understanding of the Taoist texts and for the fact that he repeatedly declined to hold official posts. After marrying off his children, he abandoned his family to visit the five famous holy mountains and never returned.

Line 4. Tao Yuanming (?–427) was a famous Chinese poet of the Jin Dynasty. He held a lowly official post for a very short time. Once, when a high official came to inspect his work, he was advised by his underlings to be very obsequious to him. It was noted in history that he sighed and said, "How could I, for only five *dou* of rice, bow down to a mean spirit?" and then left his official post. For further information see Introduction.

Deep South Mountain

Line 1. Taiyi is another name for Deep South Mountain, south of Chang'an (now the city of Xian), the capital city of the Tang Dynasty. It lies in central China, in Shaanxi province, far from the ocean. Only in the eyes of the poet, of course, do the mountains extend to the ocean.

From Dasan Pass, Going Through Shaggy Forests and Dense Bamboo, Climbing Paths Winding for Forty or Fifty Miles to Yellow Ox Peak Where I See Yellow Flower River Shining

Line 8. Whistling was said to be popular among ancient Chinese hermits as a way of achieving oneness with nature.

Stone Gate Temple in the Blue Field Mountains

Line 23. "Peach Tree Spring." See note for "Song of Peach Tree Spring" (p. 163).

From Ascetic Wang Wei to Hungry Zhang Yin

Line 16. Zhen is the cognomen of a Han Dynasty hermit, Zheng Pu, who was poor but refused constant pressure to accept official service.

Written on a Rainy Autumn Night After Pei Di's Visit

Line 5. Some Buddhist texts refer to the benevolent laws as the "white laws" and the evil laws as the "black laws."

Line 8. Qiu and Yang were ancient scholars who declined offers of official salaries and earned their own living by making carts and carriages.

Lazy About Writing Poems

Lines 7–8. When one puts Wang Wei's given name and his chosen pen name together (which reads *Wei Mojie*), it makes up the Chinese characters for the name of the Indian Buddhist sage Vimalakirti.

The Wang River Sequence and Other Poems

To Pei Di, While We Are Living Lazily at Wang River

Line 8. "Five Willows" is often used in Wang Wei's poems to represent a kind of peaceful and secluded life since Tao Yuanming, a Jin Dynasty poet of the fifth century, called himself "Master of Five Willows" after the willows that grew at his country cottage.

Living Lazily by the Wang River

Line 1. "White Group" refers to a legendary rural gathering of ancient sages. Their meeting place is supposed to be to the east of present day Luoyang.

Line 7. "Yuling," which means "at the mountain," was the name Chen Zhongzi gave to himself. This ancient sage loved country life and shunned official posts. Once the King of Chu send for him and sought his service, offering him a lot of gold, but he declined the offer, for he preferred working as a gardener to the life of an official.

Written at Wang River Estate in the Rain

Line 8. There is a Chinese fable about a young man who used to frequent the seashore and play with sea gulls. The sea gulls never flew away when he was there. When his father came to know this, he asked the young man to catch a sea gull and bring it home. The next day the young man went to the seashore with this thought in mind, but the gulls no longer would come to play with him.

A Reluctant Official at the Emperor's Court

To My Cousin Qiu, Military Supply Official

Line 13. Xie Huilian (397–433) was the valued cousin of the famous Northern and Southern Dynasties poet Xie Lingyun (385–433). Huilian was a talented young man who began to write at the age of ten. Later poets often referred to him when praising their cousins or brothers.

Winter Night, Writing about My Emotion

Line 7. Once the Han emperor Wu Di (meaning "military emperor") saw an old courtier named Yan Si and asked why he was so old but still held a low official rank. "In the time of your grandfather Wen Di [meaning "literary emperor"]," the old man answered, "I was a military man and was thus not in favor. Then your father Jing Di [meaning "emperor of scenery"] trusted only the old people and I was young. Now you like militant young people, but I am old." Wu Di was moved by this answer and raised the old man to a higher rank.

Saying Goodbye to a Friend Returning to the Mountain

Lines 9–12. The imagery in these lines is derived from legendary stories of the Taoist or Buddhist immortals as recorded in the chronicles and histories of various dynasties.

Line 16. Chan Yin was a famous fortune-teller of the Warring States Period (475–221 B.C.).

Visiting Jia's Chamber on Mount Tai Yi

Line 11. "Purple Light" refers to the realm in the sky in which the immortals live.

For Wei Mu the Eighteenth

Line 1. According to Jin History, the famous Jin Dynasty poet Ruan Ji (A.D. 210–263) would look at people or things that he disliked with the whites of his eyes (that is, with the pupils turned upward) to show his contempt. Those he was fond of he looked at with the black, or pupil, of his eyes.

Frontier Poems

Seeing Yuan Off on His Official Trip to Anxi

Title. Anxi is present-day Turfan in Xinjian, a Turkic desert region in northwest China through which the old Silk Road passed.

Line 4. Yang Pass was built in the Han Dynasty. With Jade Gate Pass, it was one of the two major strategic passes on the routes from the central part of China to its northwest. Jade Gate was to the north of Yang Pass.

Saying Goodbye to Ping Danran, Overseer

Line 8. The Yuezhi were a tribe living in the Gansu area during the early Han Dynasty. After being defeated by the Xiongnu, the Tatars, their king's skull was made into a drinking cup.

At the Frontier

Title. Wang Wei went to the border as an envoy from the court to bring gifts and congratulations to the generals there.

Line 1. *The History of the Former Han* noted that the militant nomadic tribes of the Mongolian border area called themselves the "Pride of Heaven."

Lines 5–6. "The General Defender of Qiang" and "the General Destroyer of Barbarians" are Han Dynasty titles for generals at the frontier.

Seeing Prefect Liu Off to Anxi

Lines 5–6. The horses of heaven are a special breed of horses that came from Dawan, which in the Han Dynasty was a subject nation. Alfalfa was the horses' favorite food, coming from the same region. Grapes, rare at the time, came from Xinjian.

A Tang General Sallies into the Wilderness Beyond Mount Yanzhi to Battle Against the Barbarians

Line 6. Jade Fortress—see note for line 4 of "Seeing Yuan Off on His Official Trip to Anxi" (p. 161).

Line 7. Wei and Huo refer to Wei Quing and Huo Qubing, both famous generals of the Han Dynasty.

Line 8. The General of the Two Advisors refers to another famous Han Dynasty general, Li Guangli.

Line 11. Yue was a small kingdom in the Spring and Autumn Period (770–476 B.C.). It was often bullied by its strong neighboring kingdom Wu; after Yue was defeated in a war and the king humbled, Gou Jian, king of Yue, determined to make his kingdom stronger. He was said to live in a hut and to taste dripping gall each day so that he wouldn't forget his humiliation. Eventually, he trained a good army and defeated Wu.

Line 12. This is an allusion to a well-known story about Guan Yu, a general of Shu during the Three Kingdoms Period (A.D. 221–265) who, being wounded in the arm by a poison arrow, allowed his doctor to scrape the poison from the bone without using any anesthetic, all the while drinking and talking with his fellow generals.

Line 17. "Hooks from Wu" stands for good weaponry. Wu was an ancient kingdom where, at its king's encouragement, good swords and hooks were made.

Line 20. Yuezhi bowl—see note for line 8 of "Saying Goodbye to Ping Danran, Overseer" (p. 161).

An Old General, on Long Mountain, Complains

Line 2. Mars, which in ancient China was called "the extremely white star," was a star associated with war.

Lines 9–10. These two lines allude to the story of Su Wu, a Han official who was sent by Emperor Wu Di as emissary to the Xiongnu, a tribe of the frontier regions. Refusing to be bought over, he was detained and forced to serve as a shepherd in the North Sea (now Lake Baikal). He was told that only when a goat got pregnant could he return. After nineteen years as a captive in the desert, he was released when the Han Regime and the Xiongnu came to be on better terms. On returning, the hair in the yak tail attached to his envoy's flag had all fallen out. As a reward he was made minister of the Vassal States, a lowly position not commensurate with his devotion and service.

Missing Her Husband on an Autumn Night

Title. This poem is written from the point of view of a woman, whose husband is at the frontier.

Line 1. The leaking water refers to the dripping of a waterclock.

Line 5. According to an old legend there is a cassia tree on the moon, 5,000 feet high, and a man called Wu Gang chops the tree as a punishment for seeking immortality. The tree grows whole again after each ax blow.

Departures and Separations

Seeing Prefect Yang Off to Guozhou

Line 8. The cry of the nightjar, or cuckoo, resembles the Chinese phrase *bu ru guiqu*, meaning "It's better to return."

Missing the Loved One

Line 1. Red beans are supposed to grow on a kind of very tall tree in the south. According to Chinese legend, when a soldier died in the border wars, his wife wept herself to death below such a tree. Her tears turned into red beans.

Seeing Zhao Heng Off to Japan

Title. Zhao Heng was a Japanese envoy to the early Tang dynasty and stayed to become a Chinese official for a few years.

Line 3. Nine States refers to a legendary period when China was divided into nine states.

Line 5. People of the Tang Dynasty were told by Japanese visitors that Japan was the home of the sun.

Line 9. Japan was said to be an island full of great mulberry trees, so Great Mulberry Tree became another name for Japan.

Weeping for Meng Haoran

Title. This poem is an elegy for Meng Haoran (697–740), who often wrote about nature and frontier life. He and Wang Wei are considered the greatest nature poets of the Tang Dynasty.

Lines 3 and 4. Meng Haoran used to live in Xiangyang and Caizhou.

Rice Paddies and Pomegranates

Joy in the Countryside

1. Line 3. This line alludes to an anecdote in *Zhuangzi* in which an old fisherman was attracted by the music played by Confucius on his *qin* (a Chinese zither-like instrument) and left his boat to meet him at the mound under the apricot trees where Confucius delivered his lectures. In a lengthy conversation, the fisherman criticized Confucius' teachings and suggested instead following the Tao.

1. Line 4. "Peach Tree Spring." See note for "Song of Peach Tree Spring," below.

3. Line 3. Yan Hui was one of Confucius' chief disciples. His frugality was known in the saying that while pursuing his discipline he desired no more than a handful of rice, a gourd of water, and a humble cottage.

3. Line 4. "Five Willow Man." See note for line 8 of "To Pei Di, While We Are Living Lazily at Wang River" (p. 160).

Song of Peach Tree Spring

Title. Peach Tree Spring refers to a tale by Tao Qian (also called Tao Yuanming) recounting how a fisherman lost his way and sailed into a peach grove (cf. "Written in the Mountains in Early Autumn," line 4). Curious to sail to the end of the wood, he lost all sense of time and came to a narrow opening at the foot of a mountain. He sailed through and found himself in a vast stretch of land where a people lived whose life had been cut off from the world since the Qin Dynasty (221–207 B.C.). Once the fisherman had returned home, he couldn't find his way back again.

Welcoming the Goddess

Title. The Goddess of Fish Mountain is from a Chinese myth telling the story of a goddess descending to the human world and falling in love with a young man, Shi Xuanchao, of the Three Kingdoms Period (220–280). Owing to the frequent visits of the goddess, Shi's neighbors suspected that he was having an affair with a woman and were about to send him to the court. Shi had to clarify things by saying that the woman was divine, whereupon the goddess ceased to visit him. Three years later, while traveling near Fish Mountain, the young man came upon his former goddess lover. He joined her in her chariot and never returned.

A Visit to Our Village by Governor Zheng of Guozhou

Line 3. The mirror grinder refers to a story recorded in the *Biographies of the Immortals* in which an immortal disguised himself as a mirror grinder to rescue the people in a plagued area. He charged only one *qian* for his work, and when he encountered someone with the plague he would give that person a purple pill, which would cure the disease.

Line 4. This line alludes to Chen Zhongzi, a talented person of the Warring States period (475–221 B.C.), who refused to be the prime minister of the Chu Kingdom, preferring to go off and become a hired hand watering gardens.

Line 8. "Family of Ran" refers to Ran Ji, an important literary figure of the Jin Dynasty (A.D. 265–420) who led a very poor life.

Portraits

A Drunken Poet

Line 1. Tao Qian is the other name for Tao Yuanming.

Line 21. "Five Willows." See note for line 8 of "To Pei Di, While We Are Living Lazily at Wang River" (p. 160).

The Madman of Chu

Title. The madman of Chu refers to the ancient scholar Lu Tong who, seeing the hopelessness of the political management at Chu, shunned official service by feigning madness.

Lady Xi

Title. According to an anecdote in Chinese history, Prince Li Xian, half-brother of Tang Emperor Xuanzong, was captivated by the beauty of a cake seller's wife. He gave the cake seller a lot of money to give up his wife. Although the cake seller's wife became the most favored of Prince Li's wives, she refused to speak. After a year Prince Li asked her if she still missed her former husband. When she didn't answer, the prince sent for the cake seller. When she saw him, her eyes filled with tears. It so happened that Wang Wei and other poets were there as guests and were ordered to write poems for the occasion.

Line 7. "King of Chu" alludes to a similar case in history. In the Spring and Autumn Period (770–476 B.C.), the king of Chu conquered the marquis of Xi and took his wife in marriage. Although Lady Xi became the mother of two of his sons, heirs to the throne, she would never speak a word to the king of Chu.

Lady Ban

Title. Lady Ban was one of the wives of a Han Dynasty Emperor. Because of the miscarriage of a male child she lost the emperor's favor.

Dancing Woman, Cockfighter Husband, and the Impoverished Sage

Line 2. Handan was the capital city of the ancient kingdom of Zhao, where people were known for their dancing. There is a story in *Zhuangzi* about a man who goes to Handan and, witnessing the elegant manner in which the people walk there, tries to learn to walk like them. Hard as he tries, though, he cannot learn to copy the Handan way of walking. Eventually, he becomes so confused that he forgets his own style of walking and has to crawl out of Handan.

Line 10. Zou Lu was an ancient patron of scholars. His name is found in the *Chronicles*, a famous Chinese history written in the Han Dynasty.

A Wealthy Woman of Luoyang

Line 9. Ji Lun was a wealthy man of the Jin Dynasty. He had a competition with his friends Wang Kai and Yang Xiu and many others to see who was the wealthiest, and he beat them all. During the competition the emperor gave Wang Kai a coral tree about two feet tall to help him in the competition. When the coral tree was presented to Ji Lun, he grabbed a hammer and smashed the tree. Wang Kai was extremely angry, and seeing this, Ji Lun said "No need to be angry; I'll give you compensation," and he asked his men to bring out a half-dozen even larger coral trees to give to Wang Kai.

Line 10. White Jade was the name of the favorite concubine of the king of Runan in the Song period of the Northern and Southern Dynasties (A.D. 420–479).

Line 18. "A girl from Yue" refers to Xi Shi. See note for title, "Lady Xi" (p. 164).

Meditating Beyond White Clouds

The Stillness of Meditation

Line 11. Long Whistle Tower is in the Sumen Mountains, Henan Province, where Sun Deng, a hermit of the third century A.D., lived. The name of his retreat derived from Sun Deng's whistling, which was supposed to be exceptional. Whistling was said to be very popular among the intellectuals of that time, and Sun Deng was said to whistle like chirping phoenixes.

In a Monk's Room in Spring

Line 1. *Lives of the Monks*, name of a book recording the lives of 257 famous Buddhist monks living between A.D. 67 and 519.

Line 3. The line refers to the Han Dynasty custom of presenting a jade staff carved with a mourning dove to people over eighty years old.

Line 4. The turtle is a symbol of longevity. Reference is to a story in *The Chronicle*, a famous Chinese history, of a man whose bed was for twenty years supported by turtles, who nonetheless proved to be living even after his death.

For Official Yang Who Stayed at Night at Zither Terrace and in the Morning Climbed to the Pavilion of Storing Books and Then Quickly Wrote Me a Poem

Line 4. The first emperor of the Qing Dynasty (221–207 B.C.) once visited Tai Mountain and was caught in a storm. He sought shelter beneath a pine that kept the storm from him. Later he gave the pine tree an official title.

Visiting Li Ji

Line 10. Yi Cheng is the name of a place noted for the delicious wine (often called "bamboo leaf wine") produced there.

Seeing Taoist Fang Off to the Song Mountain Region

Title. Song Mountain is located in present-day Henan Province. It is the central mountain of the five famous Chinese Mountains—Hua Mountain in the west, Tai Mountain in the east, Heng Mountain in the south, another Heng (same sound but different character in Chinese) Mountain in the north, and Song Mountain.

Line 9. Su Dan is a figure in Chinese legend who through Taoism became an immortal. According to one story, before he ascended to the sky he left a cabinet for his mother that, if she knocked on it, provided her with anything she needed.

One day out of curiosity she opened the cabinet, and a white crane flew out. After that the cabinet no longer worked. Another story is that when he became immortal, two cranes flew with him to Heng Mountain where immortals live. The allusion suggests that Fang, as a genuine Taoist, had safely arrived at Song Mountain.

Line 10. The Nine Dragon Ponds are a group of ponds on Song Mountain noted for their mysterious and fathomless depth.

Visiting the Mountain Courtyard of the Distinguished Monk Tanxing at Enlightenment Monastery

Line 2. Tiger Creek is located at Lu Mountain. According to legend, in the Eastern Jin Dynasty (A.D. 317–420) the distinguished monk Fayuan lived at Dong Lin Monastery by the side of Tiger Creek. Whenever he went beyond the creek, tigers would growl, so he never went farther than the creek when seeing friends off. One day he was walking together with Tao Yuanming (see note on line 4 of "Written in the Mountains in Early Autumn" [p. 159]) and Lu Jingxiu, a Taoist, and they were so taken by their conversation that they crossed the creek, unaware of what they were doing. Suddenly all of the tigers began to roar. The three of them laughed and went away. Later, a pavilion was built on the spot and called "Three Laughter Pavilion."

Visiting Li, A Mountain Man, and Writing This Poem on the Wall of His Home

Line 5. Han Kang was a popular herbalist who sold his medicine in the capital of Chang An. He kept his name a secret. One day a woman recognized him and revealed his name, which caused him to return to seclusion in the mountains.

Line 6. Master Xiang was a talented man who refused to hold any official posts. After marrying off his descendants he became a hermit in the mountains and never returned.

Winter Night, Facing the Snow, Thinking of the House of the Lay Buddhist Hu

Line 1. The Chinese water clock has an arrow designating the time of day or night. The last drum of the night coincides with the water clock arrow pointing to the coming of the dawn.

Line 7. In a Han dynasty tale, Yuan An stayed in his house throughout a period of blizzards and famine, unwilling to go out and beg in a time of want. An official in charge of rescue, on discovering the reason for Yuan An's remaining inside, rewarded him for his virtue.

Autumn Meditation

Line 3. Heavenly River is the Chinese phrase for the Milky Way.

Visiting Official Lu While He Was Entertaining Monks and Writing a Poem Together

Line 1. The three virtuous positions, or states, of a bodhisattva are wisdom, service, and bestowing one's own merit on others.

Line 1. The Seven Graces are the seven developments of holiness, which are said to be faith, observance of commandments, hearing instructions, shame, shame for others, renunciation, and wisdom.

Line 2. "The dark of our Eyes." See note for line 1, "For Wei Mu the Eighteenth" (p. 161).

Line 2. The lotus flower in Buddhist practice is an emblem of purity.

Line 5. This is an allusion to a line from "Wandering on Mt. Tiantai" by Sun Chuo, a fourth-century writer of *fu* (rhyme prose). The line depicts Buddhist *arhats* (saints) as "responders-to-truth, with tin staffs of flying, treading the void."

Line 10. "Five Buddhist Heavens" refers to the five highest spheres of the eighteen Buddhist heavens. They are inhabited by *arhats* who have escaped the cycle of rebirth.

Barnstone, Willis. *The Poetics of Ecstasy: Varieties of Ekstasis from Sappho to Borges*. New York: Holmes & Meier, 1983.

———, ed. with introds. *The Other Bible: Jewish Pseudepigrapha, Christian Apocrypha, Gnostic Scriptures*. San Francisco: Harper & Row, 1984.

———, ed. and trans. *Sappho and the Greek Lyric Poets*. Introduction by William E. McCulloh. New York: Schocken, 1988.

Cheng, François. *Chinese Poetic Writing*. Translated by Donald A. Riggs and Jerome P. Seaton. Bloomington: Indiana University Press, 1982.

Eliade, Mircea. *A History of Religious Ideas*. Vol. 2 *From Gautama Buddha to the Triumph of Christianity*. Chicago: University of Chicago Press, 1982.

García Lorca, Federico. "Romance Sonámbulo." In *Selected Poems*, edited by Francisco García Lorca and Donald M. Allen. New York: New Directions, 1955.

Liu Wu-Chi. *An Introduction to Chinese Literature*. Bloomington: Indiana University Press, 1966.

Machado, Antonio. *The Dream Below the Sun: Selected Poems of Antonio Machado*. Translation by Willis Barnstone. Introduction by John Dos Passos. Reminiscence by Juan Ramón Jiménez. Trumansburg, N.Y.: Crossing Press, 1981.

Owen, Stephen. *The Poetry of the Early T'ang*. New Haven, Conn.: Yale University Press, 1977.

Payne, Robert, ed. *The White Pony: An Anthology of Chinese Poetry from the Earliest Times to the Present Day, Newly Translated*. London: George Allen & Unwin, 1949.

Robinson, G. W. *Poems of Wang Wei: Translated with an Introduction*. Baltimore: Penguin, 1973.

Thomas, E. J., ed. *Early Buddhist Scriptures*. Harmondsworth, UK: Penguin, 1959.

Wagner, Marsha L. *Wang Wei*. New York: Twayne, 1981.

Waley, Arthur. *The Way and Its Power: A Study of the Tao te Ching and Its Place in Chinese Thought*. London: Allen and Unwin, 1934.

———, ed. and trans. *Three Ways of Thought in Ancient China*. New York: Macmillan, 1939.

Walmsley, Lewis, and Dorothy B. Walmsley. *Wang Wei the Painter-Poet*. Rutland, Vt.: Charles E. Tuttle, 1968.

Warren, Henry Clarke, trans. "The Fire Sermon." In *Buddhism in Translations*. Cambridge, Mass.: Harvard University Press, 1896. Reprint. Edited by Daniel H. H. Ingalls. New York: Athenaeum, 1976.

Watson, Burton. *Chinese Lyricism: Shih Poetry from the Second to the Twelfth Century, with Translations*. New York: Columbia University Press, 1971.

———, ed. and trans. *The Columbia Book of Chinese Poetry: From Early Times to the Thirteenth Century*. New York: Columbia University Press, 1984.

Wittgenstein, Ludwig. *Tractatus Logico-Philosophicus*. Translated by D. F. Pears and B. F. McGuiness. Introduction by Bertrand Russell. London: Routledge & Kegan Paul, 1961.

Wright, James. *Collected Poems*. Middletown, Conn.: Wesleyan University Press, 1971.

Yip, Wailim. *Hiding the Universe: Poems by Wang Wei*. New York: Grossman, 1972.

Yu, Pauline. *The Poetry of Wang Wei: New Translations and Commentary*. Bloomington: Indiana University Press, 1980.

Editions of Wang Wei's Poems

Chen Yixin, ed. *Wang Wei shixuan*. Beijing: Renmin, 1959.
Fu Donghua, ed. *Wang Wei shixuan*. Hong Kong: Daguang, 1973.
Gu Chijing, ed. *Leijien Wang Youcheng chuanji*. 2 vols. 1557. Reprint. Taipei, 1970.
Zhao Diancheng, ed. *Wang Youcheng ji zhu: Sibu beiyao*. 2 vols. 1736. Reprint. Taipei: Zhonghua, 1966.
———. *Wang Youcheng ji jianzhu*. 2 vols. Beijing: Zhonghua, 1961.

Translations of Wang Wei's Poems

Chang, Yin-nan, and Lewis C. Walmsley, trans. *Poems of Wang Wei*. Rutland, Vt.: Charles E. Tuttle, 1958.
Ch'eng Hsi and Henry W. Wells, trans. *An Album of Wang Wei*. Hong Kong: Ling ch'ao hsuan, 1974.
Robinson, G. W. *Poems of Wang Wei: Translated with an Introduction*. Baltimore: Penguin, 1973.
Yip, Wailim. *Hiding the Universe: Poems by Wang Wei*. New York: Grossman, 1972.
Yu, Pauline. *The Poetry of Wang Wei: New Translations and Commentary*. Bloomington: Indiana University Press, 1980.

Secondary Sources

Barnstone, Willis. *The Poetics of Ecstasy: Varieties of Ekstasis from Sappho to Borges*. New York: Holmes & Meier, 1983.
———, ed. with introd. *The Other Bible: Jewish Pseudepigrapha, Christian Apocrypha, Gnostic Scriptures*. San Francisco: Harper & Row, 1984.
Chan, Wing-tsit, ed. and trans. *A Sourcebook in Chinese Philosophy*. Princeton, N.J.: Princeton University Press, 1963.
Chang Chung-yüan. *Original Teachings of Ch'an Buddhism*. New York: Vintage, 1971.
Chaves, Jonathan. *Mei Yao-ch'en and the Development of Early Sung Poetry*. New York: Columbia University Press, 1976.

Chen, Ellen Marie. "Nothingness and the Mother Principle in Early Chinese Taoism." *International Philosophical Quarterly* 9 (1969): 391–405.

Chen Yixin (Ch'en I-hsin). "Wang Wei, the Nature Poet." *Chinese Literature*, 7 July 1962, 12–22.

Ch'en, Kenneth K. S. *Buddhism in China: A Historical Survey.* Princeton, N.J.: Princeton University Press, 1964.

——. *The Chinese Transformation of Buddhism.* Princeton, N.J.: Princeton University Press, 1973.

Cheng, François. *Chinese Poetic Writing.* Translated by Donald A. Riggs and Jerome P. Seaton. Bloomington: Indiana University Press, 1982.

Conze, Edward. *Buddhism: Its Essence and Development.* New York: Harper & Row, 1959.

——. *Buddhist Thought in India.* London: Allen and Unwin, 1962.

——, ed. *Buddhist Texts through the Ages.* Oxford: Oxford University Press, 1954. Reprint. New York: Harper & Row, 1964.

——, trans. *Buddhist Wisdom Books.* New York: Harper & Row, 1972.

Dumoulin, Heinrich. *A History of Zen Buddhism.* Boston: Beacon, 1971.

Eliade, Mircea. *A History of Religious Ideas.* Vol. 2, *From Gautama Buddha to the Triumph of Christianity.* Chicago: University of Chicago Press, 1982.

——. *Shamanism: Archaic Techniques of Ecstasy.* Translated by Willard R. Trask. Bollingen Series, no. 76. Princeton, N.J.: Princeton University Press, 1972.

Eoyang, Eugene. "The Solitary Boat: Images of Self in Chinese Nature Poetry." *Journal of Asian Studies* 32 (August 1973): 593–621.

García Lorca, Federico. "Romance Sonámbulo." In *Selected Poems.* Edited by Francisco García Lorca and Donald M. Allen. New York: New Directions, 1955.

Gong Shu. "The Function of Space and Time as Compositional Elements in Wang Wei's Poetry: A Study of Five Poems." *Literature East and West* 16 (April 1975): 1168–93.

Granet, Marcel. *La religion des Chinois.* Paris: Presses Universitaires de France, 1950.

Hightower, James Robert. *The Poetry of T'ao Ch'ien.* Oxford: Clarendon Press, 1970.

John of the Cross, Saint. *The Poems of Saint John of the Cross.* English versions and introduction by Willis Barnstone. New York: New Directions, 1968.

Lattimore, David. "Allusion and T'ang Poetry." In *Perspectives on the T'ang,* edited by Denis Twitchett and Arthur F. Wright. New Haven, Conn.: Yale University Press, 1973.

Liu, James J. Y. *The Art of Chinese Poetry.* Chicago: University of Chicago Press, 1962.

——. *The Chinese Knight-Errant.* Chicago: University of Chicago Press, 1967.

——. *Chinese Theories of Literature.* Chicago: University of Chicago Press, 1975.

Liu Wu-Chi. *An Introduction to Chinese Literature.* Bloomington: Indiana University Press, 1966.

Liu Wu-chi and Irving Y. Lo, eds. *Sunflower Splendor: Three Thousand Years of Chinese Poetry.* New York: Doubleday Anchor, 1975.

Luk, Charles, trans. *The Vimalakirti Nirdesa Sutra.* Berkeley, Calif.: Shambala, 1972.

Luk, Thomas Yuntong. "A Cinematic Interpretation of Wang Wei's Nature Poetry." *New Asia Academic Bulletin* 1 (1978): 151–61.

Luk, Yuntong. "Wang Wei's Perception of Space and His Attitude Towards Mountains." *Tamkang Review* 7 (April 1977): 89–110.

Machado, Antonio. *The Dream Below the Sun: Selected Poems of Antonio Machado.* Translation by Willis Barnstone. Introduction by John Dos Passos. Reminiscence by Juan Ramón Jiménez. Trumansburg, N.Y.: Crossing Press, 1981.

Owen, Stephen. *The Poetry of the Early T'ang.* New Haven, Conn.: Yale University Press, 1977.

Payne, Robert, ed. *The White Pony: An Anthology of Chinese Poetry from the Earliest Times to the Present Day, Newly Translated.* London: George Allen & Unwin, 1949.

Pulleyblank, E. G. *The Background of the Rebellion of An Lu-shan.* Oxford: Oxford University Press, 1966.

Robinson, G. W. *Poems of Wang Wei.* Baltimore: Penguin, 1973.

Smith, D. H. *Chinese Religions.* New York: Holt, Rinehart and Winston, 1968.

Thomas, E. J. *The Life of the Buddha as Legend and History.* London: Routledge and Kegan Paul, 1926.

Thompson, Laurence G. *Chinese Religions: An Introduction* (4th ed.). Belmont, Calif.: Wadsworth, 1989.

Twitchett, Denis, and Arthur F. Wright, eds. *Perspectives on the T'ang.* New Haven, Conn.: Yale University Press, 1973.

Wagner, Marsha L. *Wang Wei.* New York: Twayne, 1981.

Waley, Arthur. *Three Ways of Thought in Ancient China.* New York: Macmillan, 1939.

Walmsley, Lewis, and Dorothy B. Walmsley. *Wang Wei the Painter-Poet.* Rutland, Vt.: Charles E. Tuttle, 1968.

Warren, Henry Clarke, trans. "The Fire Sermon." In *Buddhism in Translations.* Cambridge, Mass.: Harvard University Press, 1896. Reprint. Edited by Daniel H. H. Ingalls. New York: Athenaeum, 1976.

Watson, Burton. *Chinese Lyricism: Shih Poetry from the Second to the Twelfth Century, with Translations.* New York: Columbia University Press, 1971.

——— , ed. and trans. *The Columbia Book of Chinese Poetry: From Early Times to the Thirteenth Century.* New York: Columbia University Press, 1984.

Welbon, Guy Richard. *The Buddhist Nirvana and Its Western Interpreters.* Chicago: University of Chicago Press, 1968.

Welch, Holmes. *Taoism: The Parting of the Way.* Boston: Beacon, 1957.

Wieger, L. *Histoires des croyances religieuses et des opinions philosophiques en Chine depuis l'origine jusqu'a nos jours.* Sienhsien, (Hokienfu): Impr. de Sienhsien, 1917.

Wittgenstein, Ludwig. *Tractatus Logico-Philosophicus.* Translated by D. F. Pears and B. F. McGuiness. Introduction by Bertrand Russell. London: Routledge & Kegan Paul, 1961.

Wolf, Arthur P., ed. *Religion and Ritual in Chinese Society.* Stanford, Calif.: Stanford University Press, 1974.

Yang, C. K. *Religion in Chinese Society.* Berkeley: University of California Press, 1967.

Yip, Wailim. *Chinese Poetry: Major Modes and Genres.* Berkeley: University of California Press, 1976.

——— . *Hiding the Universe: Poems by Wang Wei.* New York: Grossman 1972.

——— . "Wang Wei and the Aesthetic of Pure Experience." *Tamkang Review.* 2, 3 (Oct. 1971, April 1972).

Yu, Pauline. "Chinese and Symbolist Poetic Theories," *Comparative Literature*. 30 (Fall 1978): 291–312.

———. "The Poetics of Discontinuity: East-West Correspondences in Lyric Poetry." *PMLA* 94 (March 1979): 261–74.

———. *The Poetry of Wang Wei: New Translations and Commentary*. Bloomington: Indiana University Press, 1980.

———. "Wang Wei: Recent Studies and Translations." *Chinese Literature*. 1 (July 1979): 219–40.

———. "Wang Wei's Journeys in Ignorance." *Tamkang Review*. 7 (April 1977): 73–87.

———. *"The World of Wang Wei's Poetry: An Illumination of Symbolist Poetics."* Ph.D diss., Stanford University, 1976.

Library of Congress Cataloging-in-Publication Data

Wang, Wei, 701–761.
  [Poems. English. Selections]
Laughing lost in the mountains : poems of Wang Wei / translations by Tony
Barnstone, Willis Barnstone, Xu Haixin ; critical introduction by Willis
Barnstone & Tony Barnstone.
  p. cm.
Includes bibliographical references.
ISBN 0-87451-563-7. — ISBN 0-87451-564-5 (pbk.)
  1. Wang, Wei, 701–761—Translations into English. I. Barnstone, Tony.
II. Barnstone, Willis, 1927–   . III. Xu, Haixin.
IV. Title.
PL2676.A226 1991
895.1′13—dc20   ∞   91-50376